"The authors of *Applied AI* have incredible depth of expertise and experience in AI, and they make the complex topic accessible to everyone. It's rare to find technology experts as engaging and thought-provoking."

STEPHEN STRAUSS
Head of Sales Enablement and Insights, PayPal

"This book cuts the fluff and arms business leaders with exactly the right foundational knowledge to lead successful AI initiatives at their companies. It's hands down the best playbook for executives starting on their automation journey."

JACK CHUA
Director of Data Science, Expedia

"As a deep learning researcher and educator, I'm alarmed by how much misinformation and misreporting occurs with AI. It's refreshing to see a practical guide written by experienced technologists which explains AI so well for a business audience. In particular, I'm glad to see this book addresses critical issues of AI safety and ethics and advocates for diversity and inclusion in the industry."

RACHEL THOMAS
Co-Founder, fast.ai and Assistant Professor, USF Data Institute

"Full of valuable information and incredibly readable. This book is the perfect mix of practical and technical. If you're an entrepreneur or business leader, you need this guide."

JEFF PULVER
Co-Founder, Vonage and MoNage

"*Applied AI* is the perfect primer for anyone looking to understand the enterprise implications of emerging artificial intelligence technology—a must read for any business leader intending to stay ahead."

ALEX STEIN
Sr. Director, Strategy & Business Development, Viacom International Media Networks

"Recent progress in AI will dramatically impact all aspects of a business. This excellent book provides a practical examination of how to harness disruptive technologies to achieve scalable and sustainable business success."

STEVEN KUYAN
Managing Director, NYU Tandon Future Labs

Applied Artificial Intelligence

A HANDBOOK FOR BUSINESS LEADERS

Printed in the United States of America

First Printing December 2017

ISBN 978-0-9982890-2-1 (Paperback)
ISBN 978-0-9982890-5-2 (Kindle)

Edited by Natalia Zhang
Cover Illustration by Vanessa Maynard
Interior Design by Vanessa Maynard

Website: www.appliedaibook.com
Email: authors@appliedaibook.com

For all of you who build technology
to make tomorrow better than today.

TABLE OF CONTENTS

APPLIED ARTIFICIAL INTELLIGENCE

WHO THIS BOOK IS FOR

Applied Artificial Intelligence is a practical guide for business leaders who are passionate about leveraging machine intelligence to enhance the productivity of their organizations and the quality of life in their communities. If you love to drive innovation by combining data, technology, design, and people, and to solve real problems at an enterprise scale, this is your playbook.

There are plenty of technical tomes on the market for engineers and researchers who want to master the nitty-gritty details of modern algorithms and toolsets. You can also find plenty of general interest content for the public about the impact of AI on our society and the future of work.

This book is a balance between the two. We won't overload you with details on how to debug your code, but we also won't bore you with endless generalizations that don't help you make concrete business decisions. Instead, we teach you how to lead successful AI initiatives by prioritizing the right opportunities, building a diverse team of experts, conducting strategic experiments, and consciously designing your solutions to benefit both your organization and society as a whole.

How to Use This Book

The first part of this book, "What Business Leaders Need to Know," gives executives an essential education in the state of artificial intelligence today. We recommend reading this part in full before pursuing AI projects for your organization.

Chapters 1 and 2 provide a non-technical introduction to AI, the techniques used to power modern AI systems, and the functional differences between different levels of machine intelligence. While you do not need to memorize every detail, a passing familiarity with technical definitions will help you separate hype from reality when evaluating a project proposal for your own organization.

Chapters 3, 4, and 5 describe promising applications of AI in society as well as challenges that arise from biased or unethical algorithms. You'll learn how collaborative design is essential to ensuring that we build benevolent AI systems.

In the second part of our book, "How to Develop an Enterprise AI Strategy," we walk you through the strategic and methodological steps required to implement successful AI projects for your company. These chapters act as a reference guide as you are building your initiatives.

Read through them once to familiarize yourself with the content, and then refer back to specific sections as needed during your projects.

Chapters 6 and 7 teach you how to prepare your organization to succeed in AI projects. You will learn strategies to manage important stakeholders and attract technical talent.

In Chapter 8, we guide you through exercises that will help you to identify opportunities for AI adoption within your organization and develop a business plan for implementation and deployment. Chapters 9, 10, and 11 explain common technical challenges you will encounter in building AI and how to overcome them.

The last section of our book, "AI For Enterprise Functions," highlights popular AI applications for common business functions. Chapter 12 summarizes some of the challenges of adopting AI solutions for enterprises. Chapters 13 and 14 introduce common AI applications in essential administrative functions like finance, legal, and HR, while Chapters 15 and 16 describe how machine learning can dramatically improve business intelligence, analytics, and software development. Chapters 17, 18, and 19 focus on the revenue-generating functions of sales, marketing, and customer service.

Finally, Chapter 20 emphasizes the ethical responsibility that you, as business and technology leaders, have towards your workforce as well as towards ensuring that any technologies that you build have a benevolent impact on your customers, employees, and society as a whole.

Because AI technologies evolve very quickly, we created an educational website, **appliedaibook.com**, where we offer updated content and detailed case studies for specific industries. Supplemental content for this book can be found in our resources section at **appliedaibook. com/resources**.

We also created social communities and discussion forums for our readers to connect with us and each other, which you can join by visiting **appliedaibook. com/community**.

What Business Leaders
Need to Know About
Artificial Intelligence

1. BASIC TERMINOLOGY IN ARTIFICIAL INTELLIGENCE

Think about the most intelligent person you know. What about this person leads you to describe him or her this way?

Is she a quick thinker, able to internalize and apply new knowledge immediately? Is he highly creative, able to endlessly generate novel ideas that you'd never think of? Perhaps she's highly perceptive and hones in on the tiniest details of the world around her. Or maybe he's deeply empathetic and understands how you're feeling even before you do.

Human intelligence spans a wide spectrum of modalities, exhibiting abilities such as logical, spatial, and emotional cognition. Whether we are math geniuses or charismatic salesmen, we must utilize cognitive abilities like working memory, sustained attention, category formation, and pattern recognition to understand and succeed in the world every day.

Though computers trounce humans at large-scale computational tasks, their expertise is narrow, and machine capability lags behind human intelligence in other areas. The rest of this chapter will help you to understand the state of artificial intelligence today.

AI vs. AGI

Artificial intelligence, also known as AI, has been misused in pop culture to describe almost any kind of computerized analysis or automation. To avoid confusion, technical experts in the field of AI prefer to use the term Artificial General Intelligence (AGI) to refer to machines with human-level or higher intelligence, capable of abstracting concepts from limited experience and transferring knowledge between domains. AGI is also called "Strong AI" to differentiate from "Weak AI" or "Narrow AI," which refers to systems designed for one specific task and whose capabilities are not easily transferable to other systems. We go into more detail about the distinction between AI and AGI in our Machine Intelligence Continuum in Chapter 2.

Though Deep Blue, which beat the world champion in chess in 1997, and AlphaGo, which did the same for the game of Go in 2016, have achieved impressive results, all of the AI systems we have today are "Weak AI." Narrowly intelligent programs can defeat humans in specific tasks, but they can't apply that expertise to other tasks, such as driving cars or creating art. Solving tasks outside of the program's original parameters requires building additional programs that are similarly narrow.

"We're very far from having machines that can learn the most basic things about the world in the way humans and animals can," said Yann LeCun, head of AI at Facebook, in an interview with *The Verge*.[1] "In particular areas machines have superhuman performance, but in terms of general intelligence we're not even close to a rat." In addition, the path towards AGI is also unclear. Approaches that work well for solving narrow problems do not generalize well to tasks such as abstract reasoning, concept formulation, and strategic planning—capabilities that even human toddlers possess but our computers do not.

Modern AI Techniques

We are often asked to explain the key differences between machine learning, data science, AI, deep learning, etc. All of these are examples of machine intelligence, but they vary in their usage and potential impact. While engineers and researchers must master the subtle differences between various technical approaches, business and product leaders should focus on the ultimate goal and real-world results of machine learning models. This section is a guide to today's most popular techniques, but methodologies are constantly evolving. You don't need to memorize the guide, but you should try to gain a passing familiarity with the basic characteristics of each technique.

In general, most enterprise-scale technologies use a wide range of automation methodologies, but not all of them count as AI. Differentiating between methods that are AI and those that are not can be tricky, and there is often overlap. You will find that simpler approaches often outperform complex ones in the wild, even if they're intellectually less "advanced."

Though AI refers to a larger umbrella of computational techniques, the most successful modern AI solutions are powered by machine learning algorithms. For simplicity, we use AI and machine learning as interchangeable terms in this book.

STATISTICS AND DATA MINING

Statistics is the discipline concerned with the collection, analysis, description, visualization, and drawing of inferences from data. Its focus is on describing the properties of a dataset and the relationships that exist between data points. Statistics is generally not considered part of AI, but many statistical techniques form the foundation for more advanced machine learning techniques or are used in conjunction with them.

Descriptive statistics describes or visualizes the basic features of the data being studied. A simple application could be to find the best-selling retail item in a store in a specific period of time.

Inferential statistics is used to draw conclusions that apply to more than just the data being studied. This is necessary when analysis must be conducted on a smaller, representative dataset when the true population is too large or difficult to study. Because the analysis is done on a subset of the total data, the conclusions that can be reached with inferential statistics are never 100 percent accurate and are instead only probabilistic bets. Election polling, for example, relies on surveying a small percentage of citizens to gauge the sentiments of the entire population. As we saw during the 2016 US election cycle, conclusions drawn from samples may not reflect reality![2]

Data mining is the automation of exploratory statistical analysis on large-scale databases, though the term is often used to describe any kind of algorithmic data analysis and information processing, which may also include machine learning and deep learning techniques. The goal of data mining is to extract patterns and knowledge from large-scale datasets so that they can be reshaped into a more understandable structure for later analysis.

SYMBOLIC AND EXPERT SYSTEMS

Symbolic systems are programs that use human-understandable symbols to represent problems and reasoning.[3] The most successful form of symbolic systems is the expert system, which mimic the decision-making process of human experts. Expert systems are comprised of a series of production rules, similar to if-then statements, that govern how the program accesses a knowledge base and makes inferences.

Rule-based expert systems are most effective when applied to automated calculations and logical processes where rules and outcomes are relatively clear. As decision-making becomes more complex or nuanced, explicitly formalizing the full range of requisite knowledge and inference schemes required to make human-level decisions becomes impossible.

The rules engine and knowledge base for any expert system must be hand-engineered by domain experts. This is a huge drawback due to the limited number of experts who can perform the task and the time needed to program such a complicated system. The "completeness" of the knowledge base is questionable and will require continued maintenance (another huge drawback that requires enormous expenditures), and the accuracy of the system is overly-dependent on expert opinions that could be wrong. While symbolic systems are historically not scalable or adaptable, recent research has investigated combining them with newer methods like machine learning and deep learning to improve performance.

MACHINE LEARNING

What happens if you want to teach a computer to do a task, but you're not entirely sure how to do it yourself? What if the problem is so complex that it's impossible for you to encode all of the rules and knowledge upfront?

Machine learning enables computers to learn without being explicitly programmed. It is a field in computer science that builds on top of computational statistics and data mining. This book will focus primarily on discussing how machine learning is being applied in different industries across different functions, so you'll want to understand the broad categories in this field and how they are applied to business problems.

Supervised learning occurs when the computer is given labeled training data, which consists of paired inputs and outputs (e.g. an image of a cat correctly labeled as "cat"), and learns general rules that can map new inputs to the correct output. Supervised learning is commonly used for classification, where inputs are divided into discrete and unordered output categories, and for regression, where inputs are used to predict or estimate outputs that are numeric values. If you are trying to predict whether an image is of a cat or a dog, this is a classification problem with discrete classes. If you are trying to predict the numerical price of a stock or some other asset, this can be framed as a regression problem with continuous outputs.

Unsupervised learning occurs when computers are given unstructured rather than labeled data, i.e. no input-output pairs, and asked to discover inherent structures and patterns that lie within the data. One common application of unsupervised learning is clustering, where input data is divided into different groups based on a measure of "similarity." For example, you may want to cluster your LinkedIn or Facebook friends into social groups based on how connected they are to each other. Unlike supervised learning, the groups are not known in advance, and different measures of similarity will produce different results.

Semi-supervised learning lies between supervised and unsupervised learning. Many real-world datasets have noisy, incorrect labels or are missing labels entirely, meaning that inputs and outputs are paired incorrectly with each other or are not paired at all. Active learning, a special case of semi-supervised learning, occurs when an algorithm actively queries a user to discover the right output or label for a new input. Active learning is used to optimize recommendation systems, like the ones used to recommend movies on Netflix or products on Amazon.

Reinforcement learning is learning by trial-and-error, in which a computer program is instructed to achieve a stated goal in a dynamic environment. The program learns by repeatedly taking actions, measuring the feedback from those actions, and iteratively improving its behavioral policy. Reinforcement learning can be successfully applied to game-playing, robotic control, and other well-defined and contained problems. It is less effective with complex, ambiguous problems where rewards and environments are not well understood or quantified.

Chapter 10 discusses the mechanics of building machine learning models in more detail. You can also find updated technical resources on our book website, **appliedaibook.com**.

DEEP LEARNING

Deep learning is a subfield of machine learning that builds algorithms by using multi-layered artificial neural networks, which are mathematical structures loosely inspired by how biological neurons fire. Neural networks were invented in the 1950s, but recent advances in computational power and algorithm design—as well as the growth of big data—have enabled deep learning algorithms to approach human-level performance in tasks such as speech recognition and image classification. Deep learning, in combination with reinforcement learning, enabled Google DeepMind's AlphaGo to defeat human world champions of Go in 2016, a feat that many experts had considered to be computationally impossible.

Much media attention has been focused on deep learning, and an increasing number of sophisticated technology companies have successfully implemented deep learning for enterprise-scale products. Google replaced previous statistical methods for machine translation with neural networks to achieve superior performance.[4] Microsoft announced in 2017 that they had achieved human parity in conversational speech recognition.[5] Promising computer vision startups like Clarifai employ deep learning to achieve state-of-the-art results in recognizing objects in images and video for Fortune 500 brands.[6]

While deep learning models outperform older machine learning approaches to many problems, they are more difficult to develop because they require robust training of data sets and specialized expertise in optimization techniques. Operationalizing and productizing models for enterprise-scale usage also requires different but equally difficult-to-acquire technical expertise. In practice, using simpler AI approaches like older, non-deep-learning machine learning techniques can produce faster and better results than fancy neural nets can. Rather than building custom deep learning solutions, many enterprises opt for Machine Learning as a Service (MLaaS) solutions from Google, Amazon, IBM, Microsoft, or leading AI startups.

Deep learning also suffers from technical drawbacks. Successful models typically require a large volume of reliably-labeled data, which enterprises often lack. They also require significant and specialized computing power in the form of graphical processing units (GPUs) or GPU alternatives such as Google's tensor processing units (TPUs). After deployment, they also require constant training and updating to maintain performance.

Critics of deep learning point out that human toddlers only need to see a few examples of an object to form a mental concept, whereas deep learning algorithms need to see thousands of examples to achieve reasonable accuracy. Even then, they can still make laughable errors. Deep learning algorithms do not form abstractions or perform reasoning and planning in the same way that we humans do.

PROBABILISTIC PROGRAMMING

Probabilistic programming enables us to create learning systems that make decisions in the face of uncertainty by making inferences from prior knowledge. According to Avi Pfeffer in his book, *Practical Probabilistic Programming*, a model is first created to capture knowledge of a target domain in quantitative, probabilistic terms. Once trained, the model is then applied to specific evidence to generate an answer to a more specific query in a process called inference.

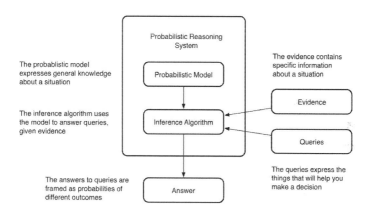

While the research and applications are in its early days, many experts see probabilistic programming as an alternative approach in areas where deep learning performs poorly, such as concept formulation using sparse or medium-sized data. Probabilistic programs have been used successfully in applications such as medical imaging, machine perception, financial predictions, and econometric and atmospheric forecasting.

Probabilistic programming is emerging as a hot area in technical research, but it has yet to be productized and operationalized for enterprise performance to the same degree that machine learning and deep learning have. We won't cover probabilistic programming in detail in this book, but you can check out the MIT Probabilistic Computing Project[7] for recommended readings and tutorials.[8]

OTHER AI APPROACHES

There are many other approaches to AI that can be used alone or in combination with machine learning and deep learning to improve performance. **Ensemble methods**, for example, combine different machine learning models or blend deep learning models with rule-based models. Most successful applications of machine learning to enterprise problems utilize ensemble approaches to produce results superior to any single model.

There are four broad categories of ensembling: bagging, boosting, stacking, and bucketing. Bagging entails training the same algorithm on different subsets of the data and includes popular algorithms like random forest. Boosting involves training a sequence of models, where each model prioritizes learning from the examples that the previous model failed on. In stacking, you pool the output of many models. In bucketing, you train multiple models for a given problem and dynamically choose the best one for each specific input.

Other techniques, such as evolutionary and genetic algorithms, are used in practice for generative design and in combination with neural networks to improve learning. Approaches like Whole Brain Uploading (WBE), also known as "mind uploading," seek to replicate human-level intelligence in machines by fully digitizing human brains. Yet other approaches seek to innovate at the hardware level by leveraging optical computing,[9] quantum computing,[10] or human-machine interfaces to accelerate or augment current methods.

The AI industry moves very quickly, and algorithms and approaches are constantly under development or being invented. To get an updated overview of modern AI technologies, download our latest guide on our book website at **appliedaibook.com/resources**.

2. THE MACHINE INTELLIGENCE CONTINUUM

If you're not an AI researcher or engineer, understanding the subtle differences and applications of various machine learning approaches can be challenging. Business problems can usually be solved in multiple ways by different algorithms, and determining the comparative merits of different methodologies can be frustrating without technical experience or practical experimentation.

To help business executives comprehend the **functional differences** between different AI approaches, we designed the Machine Intelligence Continuum (MIC) to present the different types of machine intelligence based on the complexity of their capabilities. While we've defined the continuum to contain seven levels, keep in mind that the distinction between levels is not a hard line and that many overlaps exist.

Systems That Act

The lowest level of the Machine Intelligence Continuum (MIC) contains Systems That Act, which we define as rule-based automata. These are systems that function according to some predefined script, often by following manually programmed if-then type of rules.

Examples include the fire alarm in your house and the cruise control in your car. A fire alarm contains a sensor that detects smoke levels. When smoke levels reach a predefined level, the device will play an alarm sound until it is turned off manually. Similarly, the cruise control in your car uses a powered mechanism to control the throttle position in order to maintain a constant speed.

You would never set your cruise control, take your hands off the wheel, and claim that you now have a self-driving car. Doing so would result in terrible outcomes. Yet most companies claiming to have AI are really just using Systems That Act, or rule-based mechanisms that are incapable of dynamic actions or decisions.

Systems That Predict

Systems That Predict are systems that are capable of analyzing data and using it to produce probabilistic predictions. Note that a "prediction" is a mapping of known information to unknown information and does not necessarily need to be a future event. Andrew Pole, a statistician for Target, explained to *The New York Times* that he was able to identify 25 products, including unscented lotion and calcium supplements, that can be used to predict the likelihood of a shopper being pregnant and even the stage of her pregnancy.[11] Target uses this information to serve eerily well-timed advertisements and coupons that encourage such customers to spend more money at the store.

Statistics power most Systems That Predict, but predictions are only as good as the data being used. If your data is flawed, or you choose sample data that does not sufficiently represent your target population, then you will get erroneous results. In business analysis, lack of data integrity and methodological mistakes are extremely common and often lead executives to the wrong conclusions.

Systems That Learn

While Systems That Learn also make predictions like statistical systems do, they require less hand-engineering and can learn to perform tasks without being explicitly programmed to do so. Machine learning and deep learning drive most of these systems, and they can function at human or better-than-human levels for many computational problems.

Learning can be automated at different levels of abstraction and for different components of a task. Completing a task requires first acquiring data that can be used to generate a prediction about the world. This prediction is combined with higher-level judgment to execute an action. The outcome from that action provides measurable feedback that can be reused at earlier decision points to improve task performance.

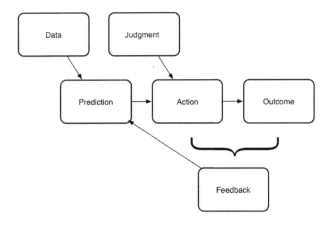

Many enterprise applications of statistics and machine learning focus on improving the prediction process. In sales, for example, machine learning approaches to lead scoring can perform better than rule-based or statistical methods. Once the machine has produced a prediction on the quality of a lead, the salesperson then applies human judgment to decide how to follow up.

More complex systems, such as self-driving cars and industrial robotics, handle everything from gathering the initial data to executing the action resulting from its analysis. For example, an autonomous vehicle must turn video and sensor feeds into accurate predictions of the surrounding world and adjust its driving accordingly.

Systems That Create

We humans like to think we're the only beings capable of creativity, but computers have been used for generative design and art for decades. Recent breakthroughs in neural network models have inspired a resurgence of computational creativity, with computers now capable of producing original writing, imagery, music, industrial designs, and even AI software![12]

Generated story about image
Model: Romantic Novels.

"He was a shirtless man in the back of his mind, and I let out a curse as he leaned over to kiss me on the shoulder.

He wanted to strangle me, considering the be-atiful boy I'd become wearing his boxers."

Image from "Generating Stories from Images" by Samim Winiger, reprinted with permission

Engineer and creative storyteller Samim trained a neural network on 14 million lines of passages from romance novels and asked the model to generate original stories based on new images.[13] Flow Machines, a division of Sony, used an AI system trained on Beatles songs to generate their own hit, "Daddy's Car," which eerily resembles the musical style of the hit British rock group. They did the same with Bach music and were able to fool human evaluators, who had trouble differentiating between real Bach compositions and AI-generated imitations.

Autodesk, the leading producer of computer-aided design (CAD) software for industrial design, released Dreamcatcher, a program that generates thousands of possible design permutations based on initial constraints set by engineers. Dreamcatcher has produced bizarre yet highly effective designs that challenge traditional manufacturing assumptions and exceed what human designers can manually ideate.

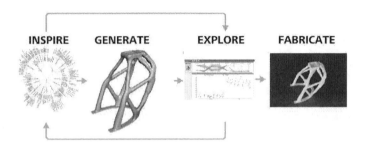

INSPIRE   GENERATE   EXPLORE   FABRICATE

Image from Autodesk Dreamcatcher, reprinted with permission

AI is even outperforming some artists economically! In 2016, Google hosted an exhibition of AI-generated art that collectively sold for $97,605.[14]

Systems That Relate

Daniel Goleman, a psychologist and author of the book *Emotional Intelligence*, believes that our emotional intelligence quotient (EQ) is more important than our intelligence quotient (IQ) in determining our success and happiness.[15] As human employees increasingly collaborate with AI tools at work and digital assistants like Apple's Siri and Amazon Echo's Alexa permeate our personal lives, machines will also need emotional intelligence to succeed in our society.

Sentiment analysis, also known as opinion mining or emotion AI, extracts and quantifies emotional states from our text, voice, facial expressions, and body language.[16] Knowing a user's affective state enables computers to respond empathetically and dynamically, as our friends do. The applications to digital assistants are obvious, and companies like Amazon are already prioritizing emotional recognition for voice products like the Echo.[17]

Emotional awareness can also improve interpersonal business functions such as sales, marketing, and communications. Rana el Kaliouby, founder of Affectiva, a leading emotion AI company, helps advertisers improve the effectiveness of brand content by assessing and adapting to consumer reactions. Mental and behavioral health is also an area ripe for innovation. Affectiva originated from academic research at MIT that was designed to help autistic patients improve recognition of social and emotional cues.[18]

Systems That Master

A human toddler only needs to see a single tiger before developing a mental construct that can recognize other tigers. If humans needed to see thousands of tigers before learning to run away, our species would have died out from predation long ago. By contrast, a deep learning algorithm must process thousands of tiger images before it can recognize them in images and video. Even then, neural networks trained on tiger photos do not reliably recognize abstractions or representations of tigers, such as cartoons or costumes.

Because we are Systems That Master, humans have no trouble with this. A System That Masters is an intelligent agent capable of constructing abstract concepts and strategic plans from sparse data. By creating modular, conceptual representations of the world around us, we are able to transfer knowledge from one domain to another, a key feature of general intelligence.

As we discussed earlier, no modern AI system is an AGI, or artificial general intelligence. While humans are Systems That Master, current AI programs are not.

Systems That Evolve

This final category refers to systems that exhibit superhuman intelligence and capabilities, such as the ability to dynamically change their own design and architecture to adapt to changing conditions in their environment. As humans, we're limited in our intelligence by our biological brains, also known as "wetware." Instead of re-architecting our own biological infrastructure during our lifetime, we evolve through genetic mutations across generations. We cannot simply insert new RAM to augment our memory capacity or install a new processor if we wish to think faster.

While we continue to search for other intelligent life, we are not yet aware of any Systems That Evolve. Computers are currently constrained by both hardware and software availability, while humans and other biological organisms are constrained by wetware limitations. Some futurists hypothesize that we may be able to achieve superhuman intelligence by augmenting biological brains with synthesized technologies, but this research is currently more science fiction than science.

Once an upgradable intelligent agent does emerge, we will reach what many experts call the technological "singularity," when machine intelligence surpasses human intelligence.[19] Self-evolving agents will be capable of ever-faster iterations of self-improvements, leading to the eventual emergence of superintelligence.

To download a visual summary of the Machine Intelligence Continuum, visit the resources section of our book website at **appliedaibook.com/resources**.

How we build today's Systems That Learn, Systems That Create, and Systems That Relate will affect how we build tomorrow's Systems That Master and Systems That Evolve. While no one can predict what superintelligence will look like, we can take measures today to increase the likelihood that the intelligent systems we design are effective, ethical, and elevate human goals and values. The next few chapters tell the story of how modern AI can be used for the good of humanity, the immediate challenges that may cause AI to go awry, and the collaborative design principles we can uphold to build the best AI systems.

3. THE PROMISES OF ARTIFICIAL INTELLIGENCE

The promises of AI extend beyond the challenges of Silicon Valley and Wall Street. Emerging technologies like deep learning and conversational interfaces enable us to do far more than drive advertising clicks, streamline sales, and boost corporate profits. All around the world, entrepreneurs and executives leverage data combined with machine learning to fight social injustice and crime, address health and humanitarian crises, solve pressing community problems, and dramatically improve the quality of life for everyone.

Microfinance

When Sahil Singla joined FarmGuide, a social impact startup, he was shocked to discover that thousands of rural farmers in India commit suicide every year.[20] When harvests fail, desperate farmers are forced to borrow from microfinance loan sharks at crippling rates. Unable to pay back these predatory loans, victims kill themselves—often by grisly methods like swallowing pesticides—to escape reprisal from their debt holders.

Singla and his team are tackling this issue with deep learning. Recent growth of computational power and structured datasets has allowed deep learning algorithms to achieve better-than-human-level accuracy in a number of recognition and classification tasks. Computers can now recognize objects in images and video, transcribe speech to text, and translate languages nearly as well as humans can.

Using deep learning, FarmGuide analyzes satellite imagery to predict crop yields for individual farms. In the US, Stanford University researchers have shown machine-driven methods for crop yield analysis to be comparably accurate to physical surveys conducted by the USDA.[21] Armed with this previously unattainable information, Singla and his team can build better actuarial models for lending and insurance, thereby reducing the risk of loan sharks preying on at-risk farmers by providing them with lower and fairer interest rates for loans.

Social Justice

In Monrovia, the capital city of Liberia, fifteen-year-old Sarafina was being hounded by one of her teachers, who refused to give her a report card unless she had sex with him. Embarrassed, she kept the issue hidden from everyone, even her parents, until her father overheard a harassing phone call that the teacher made to their home. He confronted the teacher and successfully secured Sarafina's report card, but his daughter was reprimanded and forced to move to another school.[22]

Sarafina's experience is not unique. In Liberia, teachers enjoy high social status while children, especially young girls, are culturally trained not to speak out. While Sarafina's story sounds extreme to Westerners, her experience is painfully common and largely ignored in many developing countries.

Enter UNICEF's U-Report, a social reporting bot that enables young people in developing countries to report social injustice in their communities via SMS and other messaging platforms. "U-Report is not just about getting questions answered, but getting answers back out," explains Chris Fabian, Co-Lead of UNICEF's Innovation Unit. "We get responses in real-time to use the data for policy change."[23] By using a natural language interface to capture insights and performing statistical analysis on the aggregated results, the team leverages their more than 4.2 million users worldwide to identify and tackle challenging social issues like violence against children, public health policy, and climate change.

U-Report polled 13,000 users in Liberia to ask whether teachers at their schools were exchanging grades for sex. An astonishing 86 percent of reporters said yes.[24] Within a week of the U-Report on the "Sex 4 Grades" epidemic, hotlines around the country were inundated with reports of child abuse. Simply exposing a pervasive taboo inspired many more victims to speak up and reach out for help. The outpouring of responses provoked a government response and led UNICEF and Liberia's Minister of Education to collaborate on a plan to stop the abuse of authority.

In many parts of the world, citizens can't utilize the feature-rich but data-intensive mobile apps that many of us enjoy due to bandwidth limitations and limited access to phones with up-to-date features. Being limited to voice calls and SMS means that technologies like natural language processing (NLP), dialog systems, and conversational bots become critically important to delivering value.

Medical Diagnosis

AI can dramatically streamline and improve medical care and our overall health and wellbeing. The fields of pathology and radiology, both of which rely largely on trained human eyes to spot anomalies, are being revolutionized by advancements in computer vision. Pathology is especially subjective, with studies showing that two pathologists assessing the same slide of biopsied tissue will only agree about 60 percent of the time.[25] Researchers at Houston Methodist Research Institute in Texas announced an AI system for diagnosing breast cancer that utilizes computer vision techniques optimized for medical image recognition,[26] which interpreted patient records with a 99 percent accuracy rate.[27]

In radiology, 12.1 million mammograms are performed annually in the United States, but half yield false positive results, which means that one in two healthy women may be wrongly diagnosed with cancer. In these situations, the patients often undergo biopsies, an invasive procedure that removes tissue or fluid from a suspicious area for analysis. To reduce the number of unnecessary surgical interventions, researchers at MIT and Harvard Medical School have developed a diagnostic tool that uses machine learning to correctly identify 97 percent of malignant tumors. Since deployment, the technology has reduced the number of benign surgeries by 30 percent.[28]

Artificial intelligence technologies are already saving lives and transforming societies. If used wisely, AI can be used to tackle many of the world's greatest challenges. Used unwisely, however, AI can unintentionally amplify many of humanity's worst traits. We highlight the challenges that undermine benevolent AI in the next chapter.

4. THE CHALLENGES OF ARTIFICIAL INTELLIGENCE

"The future is already here—it's just not evenly distributed."
—William Gibson

When Timnit Gebru attended a prestigious AI research conference in 2016, she counted six black people in the audience out of an estimated 8,500 attendees. There was only one black woman: herself. As a PhD from Stanford University who has published a number of notable papers in the field of artificial intelligence, Gebru finds the lack of diversity in the industry to be extremely alarming.[29]

Data and technology are human inventions, ideally designed to reflect and advance human values. As our creations grow exponentially more powerful and their footprint ever larger on our society, we need to be increasingly mindful of the need to build them to be robust against adverse and unintended consequences.

We cannot blindly trust the output of automated systems without vetting the accuracy of both the input data and the decision-making process itself. Many machine learning algorithms already influence our daily decisions and actions, but bad data and methodological mistakes can easily lead to erroneous results. In California, a flight-risk algorithm in use by the San Francisco Superior Court mistakenly recommended a man for release before trial. Despite multiple previous probation violations and arrests for gun possession, the algorithm judged him to be a minimal flight risk because someone had mis-entered the number of days that he had already spent in jail. Five days after release, he and a partner shot a local photographer.[30]

More subtle and insidious is the danger that algorithms designed by an undiversified team of elites may overlook the needs and values of underrepresented groups and unintentionally amplify the discrimination against them. Amazon customers, for example, discovered that same-day delivery was unavailable in zip codes that contained predominantly black neighborhoods, while computer scientists at Carnegie Mellon found that women were less likely than men to be shown ads for high-paying jobs.[31] Even if characteristics such as race, religion, gender, or ethnicity are eliminated from models, other features that are highly correlated with those characteristics may be included and introduce the same bias.

The biases of technology creators trickle down to their creations. While AI researchers pride themselves on being rational and data-driven, they can be blind to issues such as racial or gender bias or ethical issues that aren't easily captured by numbers. With AI now used in high-stakes systems to identify terrorists, predict criminal recidivism, and triage medical cases, homogenous thinking in the technology industry has dangerous implications.

The Effects of Discrimination

To Latanya Sweeney, the first black woman to receive a PhD in computer science from MIT, the shortcomings of AI come as no surprise. Currently a professor at Harvard and the director of their Data Privacy Lab, Sweeney's research examines technological solutions to societal, political, and governance challenges. One of her important contributions illuminates discrimination in online advertising, where she discovered that online searches of names that are more associated with the black community are 25 percent more likely to be targeted by ads that implies the person being searched for has a criminal record.[32] Sweeney also uncovered SAT test prep services that charge zip codes with high proportions of Asian residents nearly double the average rate, regardless of their actual income.[33] While price discrimination based on race, religion, nationality, or gender is illegal in the United States, enforcement of existing law is challenging in e-commerce, where the evidence of differential pricing is obscured by opaque algorithms.

In healthcare, AI systems are at risk of producing unreliable insights even when algorithms are perfectly implemented, because the availability of medical data is affected by social inequality. Poorer communities lack access to digital healthcare, which leaves a gaping hole in the medical information that is fed into AI algorithms. Randomized control trials often exclude groups such as pregnant women, the elderly, or those suffering from other medical complications.[34] Such exclusions mean that the unique physical characteristics of these patients are not incorporated into studies, which in turn affects whether tested treatment will be effective on patients who don't share the characteristics of the original clinical volunteers. In the worst-case scenario, the treatment may actively harm the patient.

Advocacy for algorithmic fairness cannot solely be the responsibility of the disenfranchised. Lasting, fundamental changes can only happen when technology creators and the public at large awaken to the dangers of exclusion and make inclusion a true priority.

Malicious AI

We don't have to wait for AI to gain sentience and go rogue, because the probability of bad people taking advantage of intelligent automation for evil purposes is 100 percent. As machine intelligence becomes more powerful, pervasive, and connected, embedding AI in all of our personal and industrial computing devices increases the risk of attacks that can compromise the security infrastructures that protect our resources and communities.

Luminaries from the Future of Humanity Institute, OpenAI, Centre for the Study of Existential Risk, and leading universities in the US and UK issued a 100-page policy recommendation paper, "The Malicious Use of Artificial Intelligence,"[35] in which they described the fast-evolving threat landscape, identified key areas of security risk, and made high-level recommendations for preventative action that should be taken immediately.

The report was alarming, pointing out that existing threats will get worse while new threats of an unknown nature will almost certainly emerge. AI will be used to multiply the effects of a malicious campaign—augmenting "human labor, intelligence, and expertise" to make the process of attacking easier and faster—and to broaden the types and number of possible targets. Advances in neural network algorithms that can produce hyperrealistic audiovisual input may be hijacked to produce fake news that looks like it came from a credible source, or to circumvent security systems that use voiceprints or other identifying features. In addition, AI may fundamentally alter the arena of cyber attacks by increasing the efficacy, precision, and untraceability of such attacks. These attacks may even target and hijack supposedly secure AI systems by exploiting their vulnerabilities. One grim possibility is the deployment of autonomous weapons systems, such as a drone, using facial recognition technology to identify and attack individuals in a crowd.

Through wearables, standard computing devices, and the burgeoning Internet of Things (IoT), AI will inevitably permeate every corner of our existence. This means that our physical security, digital security, and even political security will be at risk of attack. While we spend much of our productive hours tethered to digital devices and roaming cyberspace, we still inhabit physical bodies and live in a material world. Nefarious AI can infect autonomous vehicles, connected appliances, and other devices to inflict bodily harm and property damage. Digital attacks may come as a coordinated and adversarial disruption of corporate data with the goal of compromising, devaluing, or altogether destroying an organization's data architecture. Finally, the use of technology—including AI, predictive analytics, automation, and social media bots—can have far-ranging social impact. AI can be used for illegal surveillance, propaganda, deception, and social manipulation.

5. DESIGNING SAFE AND ETHICAL AI

Ethics and Governance

AI systems can't simply be programmed to complete their core tasks. They must be designed to do so without unintentionally harming human society. As AI systems become more complex, the likelihood of facing ethical dilemmas also grows. Designing safe and ethical AI is a monumental challenge and a critical one to tackle now. To be effective, we must develop more sophisticated and nuanced policies that go far deeper and wider than simplistic, science fiction solutions like Asimov's Three Laws of Robotics.[36]

In a joint study, Google DeepMind and the Future of Humanity Institute explored fail-safe mechanisms for shutting down rogue AI.[37] In practical terms, these "big red buttons" will be signals that trick the machine to make an internal decision to stop, without registering the input as a shutdown signal by an external human operator. IEEE, the world's largest association of technical professionals, published *Ethically Aligned Design,* a set of standards for the ethical design of artificial intelligence and autonomous systems.[38] The publication lays out the chain of accountability for design and operation. It also emphasizes that to limit the possible extent of risks, such systems should not infringe on human rights, and their operations should be transparent to a wide range of stakeholders.

Hypothetical fail-safe mechanisms and hopeful manifestos are important, but they are insufficient for addressing the myriad of ways in which AI systems can go awry.

Homogeneous development teams, insular thinking, and lack of perspective lie at the root of many of the challenges already manifesting in AI development today. Luckily, as AI education and tools become more accessible, product designers and other domain experts are increasingly empowered to contribute to a field that was previously reserved for academics and a niche community of experts.

Education as Remedy

Tackling these challenges requires democratizing access to quality AI education and empowering collaborations between practitioners and multidisciplinary experts in order to gather missing data and build inclusive technology. Acquiring the requisite knowledge and resources to apply AI is a huge challenge for those who don't live in Silicon Valley or other major research hubs.

Many turn to massive open online courses (MOOCs) provided by companies such as Coursera, Udacity, and fast.ai as their only options.

Rachel Thomas, a deep learning researcher with a doctorate in math from Duke University, started fast.ai with Jeremy Howard, the former president of Kaggle, to advance the mission of making deep learning accessible to all. As passionate champions of diversity and inclusion, the two have taught over 50,000 students globally, including Sahil Singla of FarmGuide.

Fast.ai's non-stop efforts to democratize AI education are paying off. Students of its MOOC are using techniques taught in the class to treat Parkinson's disease, give visually impaired patients more independence, fight online hate speech, and end illegal logging and harmful human activity in endangered rainforests.

The work is not done, however. Even with MOOCs, students in developing countries face an uphill battle compared to their counterparts in developed countries. Some struggle with the lack of structured datasets available in their language or culture, others with the lack of reliable internet infrastructure and access. Still others face a lack of career opportunities. Finally, the lack of affordable access to computational resources, such as graphic processing units (GPU) and reliable power sources, presents a major obstacle for students who want to build their own models. Even with the right hardware, complex neural network models can take days, if not weeks, to train.

Even if computational resources were widely available, engineering education alone is insufficient to ensure that AI technologies are built safely and successfully. "Ethics training should be a mandatory part of engineering and computer science education," emphasizes Rana el Kaliouby, founder of Affectiva, a company that makes machines more emotionally intelligent.[39] El Kaliouby and her team regularly engage the public in open dialogue to uncover potential blind spots regarding transparency, privacy, security, and ethical concerns.

Improving access to tools and education will bring in new expertise and viewpoints that can help evolve a field traditionally driven by an elite few. With AI's exponential impact on all aspects of our lives, this collaboration will be essential to developing technology that works for everyone, every day.

Collaborative Design

As you embark on building your own AI technologies for your business or community, the following three principles of collaborative design will help you and your team approach AI development more holistically and successfully. Bringing in diverse expertise and thinking is critical to ensuring your technology is benevolent to all members of society and does not unconsciously reflect the biases of an elite minority.

BUILD USER-FRIENDLY PRODUCTS TO COLLECT BETTER DATA FOR AI

Data is a human construct, as are the tools that we design to gather it. Consumer-facing digital data is largely captured through the myriad of touch points that we have with our internet-connected devices and the complex ecosystem of apps, content, and networks that we access through them. If the products collecting requisite data to power AI systems do not encourage the right types of engagement, then the data generated from user interactions tend to be incomplete, incorrect, or compromised.

In designing a product, you are building a specific journey for your customers to experience, and you will invariably influence user behavior and the resulting data trail. Manipulative products like clickbait headlines and aggressive calls-to-action (CTAs) optimize for short-term gains in lieu of long-term relationships, and the data they collect may not serve your ultimate business goals. Even if you are intentional in both your data collection and your product's user experience (UX) design, remember that just because a user engaged with a button or clicked on an ad doesn't mean you know their motives or intentions.

The absence of experiential knowledge means that you cannot solely rely on data and algorithms to tell you which problems need solving. Machine learning and AI are not always the right solutions to a problem. Identifying the right problem and its solution requires tight integration and adaptation between your products and your users as well as a collaborative relationship between your team and your users. The UNICEF U-Report bot is a great example of this principle in action. Its key innovation was in designing the product to work over a single phone line for users who lacked smartphones and computers, not in its application of novel AI methodologies.

PRIORITIZE DOMAIN EXPERTISE AND BUSINESS VALUE OVER ALGORITHMS

When working with Fortune 500 companies looking to reinvent their workflows with automation and AI, we often hear this complaint about promising AI startups: "These guys seem really smart, and their product has a lot of bells and whistles. But they don't understand my business."

In most cases, having and using a fantastic machine learning algorithm is less important than deploying a well-designed user experience (UX) for your products. Thoughtful UX design that delights users will drive up engagement, which in turn increases the interactions you can capture for future data and analysis.

Thoughtful UX compensates for areas where AI capabilities may be lacking, such as in natural language processing (NLP) for open-domain conversation. In order to develop "thoughtful UX," you'll need both strong product development and engineering talent as well as partners who have domain expertise and business acumen. A common pattern observed in both academia and industry engineering teams is their propensity to optimize for tactical wins over strategic initiatives. While brilliant minds worry about achieving marginal improvements in competitive benchmarks, the nitty-gritty issues of productizing and operationalizing AI for real-world use cases are often ignored. Who cares if you can solve a problem with 99 percent accuracy if no one needs that problem solved? What's the utility of a tool whose purpose is so arcane that no one is sure what problem it was trying to solve in the first place?

EMPOWER HUMAN DESIGNERS WITH MACHINE INTELLIGENCE

"Tools are not meant to make our lives easier," says Patrick Hebron, author of *Machine Learning For Designers*, "[t]hey are meant to give us leverage so that we can push harder. Tools lift rocks. People build cathedrals."[40] Human designers can enhance their creations when they are supported by tools that use machine intelligence. The nascent field of AI design is one such area. While we are still figuring out which best practices should be preserved and which new ones need to be invented, many promising AI-driven creative tools are already in use.

Hebron insists that machine learning can be used to simplify design tools without limiting creativity or removing control from human designers. Machine learning can transform how people interact with design tools through emergent feature sets, design through exploration, design by description, process organization, and conversational interfaces. Hebron believes that these approaches can streamline the design process and enable human designers to focus on the creative and imaginative side of the process instead of on technical mastery of the design software. This way, "designers will lead the tool, not the other way around."

How to Develop an
Enterprise AI Strategy

6. BUILD AN AI-READY CULTURE

You may have brilliant ideas for using artificial intelligence to improve your organization and community, but translating those ideas into viable software requires having the right mindset, dedicated leadership, and a diverse support team.

In this chapter, we highlight many of the organizational and political issues that routinely block technical innovation and give you strategies for overcoming them.

Be Honest About Your Readiness

Despite many public claims to innovation, many corporations are still playing catch up on existing technologies such as big data, mobile, and the Internet of Things (IoT). Many brands have built up their social media presence and now offer mobile-friendly apps and websites, but these are merely digital consumer endpoints, not the basis for an enterprise-wide technological transformation. Other companies have accumulated big piles of data, but aren't actively transforming their information assets into improved business practices.

DO YOU HAVE A CENTRAL TECHNOLOGY INFRASTRUCTURE AND TEAM?

A key milestone in the corporate digital transformation is the development of a centralized data and technology infrastructure. These two elements connect consumer applications, enterprise systems, and third-party partners and provide access to a single source of truth that contains relevant, up-to-date, and accurate information for all parties.

Designing and implementing the infrastructure needed for enterprise-scale AI requires a strong and dedicated technology team that can develop internal application programming interfaces (APIs) to standardize access to both data and your company's internal business technology. Doing so will enable your company to streamline enterprise-wide data analysis, accelerate product development, and respond more quickly in evolving markets. Internal APIs will also reduce the communication overhead needed to hunt down specific data, negotiate access, and interpret variations. You will also avoid duplicating software development work across different departments that have overlapping needs and goals.

Non-technical companies typically see technology as a secondary priority and leave software projects to siloed business units. This leads to technical sprawl, which manifests when different business units implement their own initiatives without consulting each other, build conflicting or incompatible solutions, compromise security due to inconsistent standards and access, and overload IT departments that struggle to monitor and manage everything. If your company has not yet succeeded in managing technical sprawl (or if you have not yet begun to tackle the problem), we recommend that you tackle that problem before trying to launch a complex AI initiative. If unaddressed, technical sprawl will lead to your company investing in fits and starts and buying third-party AI products for narrow purposes, which will only exacerbate your existing problem.

Building and maintaining a strategic, centralized, and secure architecture also requires strong executive commitment led by the C-Suite, plus ongoing operational collaboration from all departments and business units.

DOES YOUR CORPORATE CULTURE VALUE DATA AND ANALYTICS?

There is no point in laboriously gathering data and running sophisticated machine learning models if the analysis will be ignored. Many of the world's largest enterprises have historically grown through gut decisions from influential executives, not from collaborative, data-driven decision-making. Due to past successes, some leaders prioritize their own beliefs and methods and are openly hostile to analytical approaches and centralized technology.

Almost all of us have worked with colleagues with dogmatic qualities in our professional careers. They have a special name: HiPPO, which stands for "highest paid person's opinion." HiPPOs insist that their strategy is the right direction for the company, based largely on the fact that they came up with the idea. They often emerge with little warning to ram a new "vision" through the company or to shoot down initiatives that they perceive to be competing with their agendas. Executives who exhibit such behaviors rarely mean to be malicious and do not recognize themselves to be HiPPOs, preferring to style themselves as being "experienced" or "visionary."

Intuition-driven approaches may have worked in a bygone business era when no one had access to data or computing. However, now that software has eaten the world,[41] fortune favors the nerds. In the 15 years between 2002 and 2017, the top five publicly-traded companies by market cap shifted from GE, Microsoft, Exxon, Citi, and Walmart to technology companies like Apple, Alphabet, Microsoft, Amazon, and Facebook. While data alone cannot make decisions for you, combining the right information with experience, creativity, and an unbiased perspective will enable executives to make better decisions.

Nearly every company has a few executive HiPPOs. While you can probably manage a handful of naysayers, your company is unlikely to be competitive in AI if you're up against a HiPPO army or an extremely powerful C-Suite HiPPO. We have seen data and analytics initiatives at major companies severely hindered or even cancelled by antagonistic executives.

Choose the Right Champions

Who should own AI initiatives at your company? One pattern stands out clearly: in every single tech firm that currently leads in AI, the CEO has come out strongly in favor of prioritizing AI company-wide. Microsoft CEO Satya Nadella describes AI as being "at the intersection of our ambitions. We want to democratize AI just like we brought information to your fingertips."[42] Sundar Pichai, CEO at Google, boldly stated that "we will move from mobile first to an AI first world."[43] Amazon's Jeff Bezos calls our modern times the "golden age" of AI, stating that "we are now solving problems with machine learning and artificial intelligence that were in the realm of science fiction for the last several decades."[44]

CEO, CTO, CIO, CDO, OR CAO?

Finding the right stakeholder to champion a high-risk, high-reward technology initiative is half the battle. In a company that is traditionally conservative towards technology and digital investments, you may have a hard time convincing your CEO to champion AI initiatives. If that's the case, try to find executive buy-in as high up as possible, ideally within the C-Suite or even at the board level.

Successful enterprise AI applications can be led by many different executive roles, but whoever leads can't simply rely on aspirational press releases. True leadership has to be demonstrated through vision, action, and budget. The executive should also possess high levels of technical sophistication, including the ability to understand—or the willingness to learn—the nuances and challenges of developing data, analytics, and machine learning products.

"We've had a few people tell us that the biggest predictor of whether a company will successfully adopt machine intelligence is whether they have a C-Suite executive with an advanced math degree," says Shivon Zilis, an experienced investor in AI and a partner at Bloomberg Beta. "These executives understand it isn't magic—it is just (hard) math."[45]

The ideal characteristics of an executive AI champion include:

- C-Suite executive level or higher
- Business and domain expert
- Credible and influential

- Technically knowledgeable
- Analytical and data-driven
- Controls sufficient budget
- Encourages experimentation
- Understands and accepts risks
- Collaborates well with decision-makers across multiple business units

CEO

In an ideal world, the CEO and the Board of Directors recognize the rising importance of AI and automation everywhere. As a result, they have empowered your executives with the decision-making capability, financial budget, and organizational resources to succeed. More importantly, they are technically savvy enough to understand the risks involved and are committed to driving progress.

Leading technology CEOs have virtually all committed to the importance of AI for their businesses in public, but we've found that CEOs of non-technology companies can get caught up with existing strategy initiatives and lose traction on AI efforts. While you should always strive to have your CEO's blessings, you may want to concentrate on finding a C-Suite champion who can dedicate substantial time to shepherding AI investments to fruition.

CTO

Chief Technology Officers create technology for an enterprise's external business or individual customers. The CTO defines the technology architecture, runs engineering teams, and continuously improves the technology behind the company's product offerings. Creativity, technical skill, and ability to innovate are essential to a CTO's success.

With technology products increasingly dependent on machine learning approaches to improve performance, a company that primarily produces software will need its CTO to prioritize investments in AI. For years now, Google, Facebook, Amazon, Microsoft, and other large technology corporations have prioritized integrating machine learning into their customer-facing products, as have leading companies in virtually every sector.

Companies that don't traditionally build end-user technology often don't have CTOs, which can make transitions challenging if they want to create digital experiences for customers without relying on external agencies.

CIO

Chief Information Officers manage technology and infrastructure that underpin their company's business operations. The CIO runs an organization's IT and Operations to streamline and support business processes. Unlike the CTO, the CIO's customers are internal users, functional departments, and business units. CIOs typically adapt and integrate third-party infrastructure solutions to meet their unique business needs and do less custom development than CTOs do.

For non-technology companies, the CIO can be the right stakeholder if the primary benefits of adopting AI lie in improving analytics and business operations rather than in functions that affect external customers, such as in sales and marketing. However, in companies that view the CIO as "the IT guy" who has to report to another executive, the better stakeholder may be the higher-level executive who owns the final business decisions.

Regardless of whether they are your primary AI champion, CIOs will likely play a vital role in implementing AI in an organization due to the need to develop and integrate infrastructure to support AI. ML systems and data mining systems require complex storage, networking, and computing systems that will require the CIO's input to implement in many enterprises.

CDO

Since data touches all aspects of enterprises, Chief Data Officers (CDOs) are becoming increasingly common,[46] but their mandate is more often the security, regulation, and governance of enterprise data. Depending on their focus, they typically report to CIOs, CFOs, Chief Risk Officers (CRO), or Chief Security Officers (CSO). Companies that have the CDO report directly to the

CEO tend to value data and analytics more highly than those that don't.

Many enterprises started investing in centralized data infrastructure and capabilities less than five years ago, which means many new CDOs are still occupied with the monumental task of laying out their company-wide data initiatives. Consequently, they may not be able to focus on championing new AI investments.

For some businesses, it may make more sense to appoint a Chief Data Supply Officer (CDSO) or comparable role to support the CDO. This person can direct a company's data towards the end goal of adopting machine learning. They consider questions such as how best to manage competing sources of data, the cost of access and of data churn, where to store data, and how to simplify access to data.[47]

CAO

Along with the CDO, the Chief Analytics Officer (CAO) is a relatively new role that has emerged to manage enterprise investment in big data and analytics. Companies that are early in the maturity cycle for big data may still be working to integrate, clean, organize, prepare, and transform data into an institutional asset. Once a CDO or comparable leader has organized high-quality data, a CAO can then apply meaningful analytics to solve business problems. The roles overlap, and the titles are often interchangeable.

Many mature companies also combine the two roles so that a single executive is responsible for both the enterprise data management and the ensuing analytical functions. Corporations that see analytics as a critical asset will often have the CAO reporting directly to the CEO rather than to the CTO or CIO.

Other Important Roles
The roles that we highlighted tend to be executives with sufficient technical expertise, organizational resources, and enterprise clout to lead major AI initiatives. However, successful investments can be led by a myriad of roles including Chief Digital Officers, Chief Security Officers / Chief Information Security Officers, Chief Risk Officers, Chief Innovation Officers, Chief Science Officers, Chief Strategy Officers, etc. The exact scope and role of these positions in the C-Suite hierarchy can vary widely across organizations, so you'll need to clarify their responsibilities within your own organization before pitching them to be your champion.

AI initiatives can also be led by CMOs, COOs, CFOs, or other corporate leaders who own business decisions and maintain significant political influence within their organizations.

DO YOU NEED A CHIEF AI OFFICER?

"A hundred years ago electricity transformed countless industries; 20 years ago the internet did, too. Artificial intelligence is about to do the same," writes Andrew Ng, former Stanford University Professor of Computer Science and a widely respected technical expert on machine learning.[48] Just as CIOs became needed with the rise of the Internet and CDOs became needed with the increasing importance of data, Ng proposes that organizations establish a new role, the Chief AI Officer (CAIO), to govern and champion the role of AI in enterprises.

Is a CAIO necessary? At the time of this writing, less than three dozen professionals on LinkedIn report having this title. Ng states the primary benefit of having CAIOs is that they can centralize a powerful AI team that can build and use AI technology to accelerate and streamline business functions across an organization, not just in siloes. "Let's say your company has a gift card division," Ng uses as an example. "Because AI talent is extremely scarce right now, it is unlikely that they will attract top talent to work on gift cards at the division level. A dedicated AI team has a higher chance of attracting AI talent and maintaining standards."

Unfortunately, these benefits only accrue if you hire the right person, which is a non-trivial task. Not only do successful CAIOs need to be masters of AI and data infrastructure technologies, they must be able to collaborate effectively with different departments and different roles, understand their priorities when formulating solutions to business problems, be charismatic enough to win support for new initiatives, and have enough industry clout to attract highly sought-after talent to their teams.

AI is not a magical solution that instantaneously solves all challenges. Different, often simpler, approaches can also drive many improvements and advancements. Unless your technology initiatives are driven by clear business goals and viability, you run the risk of using AI aimlessly, like a hammer looking for nails. Deploying AI successfully also requires that your organization be "AI-ready," i.e. have a strong culture of data-driven decision-making and technical experimentation. Otherwise, even the most brilliant CAIO in the world won't do your company any good.

GET BOARD LEVEL BUY-IN

Many times, major investment projects will require board-level buy-in. A shift in company culture is often difficult when public companies are slaves to investors who expect quarterly results. Quarterly performance goals create pressure to drive toward short-term initiatives.

For example, retail brands may recognize the need to completely evolve the way they sell to customers to compete with technology entrants like Amazon, but they will likely fumble when these strategic changes require major, longer-term R&D investments.

In the face of exponential change ushered in by AI, companies need to prioritize longer-term investments for both growth and survival. These sweeping changes and resource allocations typically require board-level buy-in. While board members are not part of the executive team, they exert significant sway in shaping strategic corporate initiatives, inspiring or forcing the company to make technology investments. They can also provide support to public company leadership who are especially subject to the whims of quarterly earnings reports. Keeping your board educated and updated is essential if you aspire to larger projects.

Build An Enterprise-Wide Case For AI

Your case for investing in AI and in automation will depend on your champions and stakeholders since they possess different business priorities, performance metrics, technical aptitude, propensity for risk, and political relationships.

Presenting a clear ROI on AI initiatives is the best way to persuade executive stakeholders, but this can be challenging when enterprise AI adoption is early and still being proven in many sectors. Many corporations are still completing their big data investments and have yet to broach analytics. We emphasized earlier the importance of being honest about whether or not your organization is ready for AI. Enterprises early in the maturity cycle for big data and analytics may need to wait until a basic data and analytics infrastructure is in place before chasing AI.

If you're unable to secure executive champions right away, you may still be able to pull off a limited pilot or prototype within your own department or team. Pilot costs vary widely depending on scope, scale, application, and timeline. A short, proof-of-concept marketing project for an e-commerce company that uses an off-the-shelf solution may cost tens of thousands of dollars and be implemented in days. A more fleshed-out project, such as the codification of regulatory contracts for an investment bank, may cost millions and require years. A repository of clean, accessible data will help drive down project costs and time.

Read part three, "AI for Enterprise Functions," to develop ideas for how AI can be beneficial for your business. In this section, we highlight popular applications for internal operations like finance, legal, and HR, as well as customer-facing functions like sales, marketing, and customer service.

Why You Need a Multi-Disciplinary "AI SWAT Team"

Executives alone cannot bring about organizational change, especially of the magnitude that AI can potentially make across an enterprise and industry. Some of your most important stakeholders are your front-line employees and middle managers who will be integrating, using, and overseeing AI tools every day.

Many of your employees likely have a strong fear that AI and automation will take away their jobs. Unlike you, they may not initially understand how these powerful technologies can be used to eliminate their lower-value tasks, free them to perform creative and strategic work, and thus augment their output. We have seen firsthand how failure to educate, include, and adapt to these important voices within an organization can lead to resistance, political infighting, and internal sabotage.

You will need to put together a multi-disciplinary, cross-departmental "AI SWAT Team" composed of stakeholders in different departments, different functional roles, and different hierarchical levels. The responsibility of this team will be to support your champion and to identify, prioritize, execute, and evangelize your highest-ROI opportunities for automation across the whole company. They will also be critical for identifying potential pitfalls in your organizational design, technical capabilities, and strategic and tactical plans. These diverse views will be critical to help you and your champions form a clearer and fuller picture of the true impact of machine intelligence in your company.

Nearly every job function is now touched by technology that can benefit from machine learning, and new roles will emerge due to new computing capabilities. Therefore, while your "AI SWAT Team" will be comprised of a small group of programmers, planners, and sponsors, the team should be also surrounded by advisors from non-technical departments, such as HR or Finance, who can inform you of the areas in most urgent need of automation and the areas with the highest ROI. Coordination across departments and functions will also enable you to identify commonalities that can be addressed by machine learning and tackle them with centralized rather than siloed solutions. The size of your SWAT team may vary depending on the size of your organization but typically ranges from five to fifteen members. The membership may rotate as you mature as a digital organization and face different challenges in your evolution.

Thus far, the discussion assumes that your organization is already willing to take a stab at investing in AI. But what if it's resistant to the idea? How can you convince your organization that AI is a good idea in the first place?

Get Organizational Buy-In

Most AI implementations are cross-functional and require input from multiple departments. A retooling of your accounts payable system will need inputs from finance, legal, security, and technology. A project may also pull in human resources, if employees need to be reassigned, and operations, if processes require adjustments. To succeed, you will need support from other executives, their front-line managers, and their staff. Here are some things that you can do to win support from your organization.

Focus on Revenue Potential

A key strategy is to appeal to your business leaders about the potential of increasing the bottom line. AI can save time and energy, reduce costs, and increase profits, which then provide executives an opportunity to grow their business lines and advance their careers.

Stay Ahead of the Competition

The fear of missing out (FOMO) is also a very strong motivating force. If business unit leaders fail to take action, emphasize that they are setting themselves up to fall behind competitors who are jumping on new technology. Not investing in the organizational and technical requirements to adopt AI may mean falling so far behind that you're unable to compete in the future.

Start Small and Show Early Wins

Pick a smaller, sure-win project to demonstrate possibilities. While returns may be limited, an early success will give you confidence when you request that the project scope be expanded. Aim for something with a short time horizon that can be completed with a small task force. For example, in customer care, Nuance recommends routing a tiny portion of customer support queries to an AI system at the onset. Initially, an automated support system can answer 20 to 30 percent of frequently asked questions, but accuracy can increase to over 80 percent and expand to more topics as the system learns over time.[49]

Don't Call It Artificial Intelligence
When pitching your project, emphasize the value that new technology can deliver instead of the technical details of implementation. Karl Bunch, former SVP of Xaxis, a subsidiary of WPP, built a prototype of an algorithmic adtech trading platform with a small team of engineers working in their spare time. To keep expectations low, he refused to describe the technology as "machine learning" or "artificial intelligence" until after the system started showing great promise after a few quarters. What started out as a skunkworks project has now become a core part of Xaxis's ad tech trading platform.

Allay Fears of Sudden Job Loss
Given the negative media hype surrounding AI, your employees understandably have concerns over their job security. You can allay these fears and promote a healthy work environment in which both humans and machines cooperate and thrive. Research finds that while 45 percent of tasks are automatable, only five percent of overall jobs have been supplanted by automation.[50] AI systems largely handle individual tasks, not whole jobs.

High costs, legal regulations, and social resistance to AI all hinder the progress of technology adoption. With the rise of autonomous vehicles, many believe that the jobs of America's 1.7 million truck drivers are in imminent danger. The reality is that trucking jobs will likely require many years to replace. Michael Chui, a McKinsey partner, told *The New York Times* that the replacement and retrofitting of America's truck fleet with autonomous navigation will require a trillion-dollar investment that few, if any, companies will immediately undertake.[51] Even if financing can be secured, autonomous vehicle technology is not yet approved for industrial or for individual use.

If humans can outsource repetitive and mundane tasks to AI, then they can devote more attention to tasks requiring strategic skills such as judgment, communication, and creative thinking. Eliminating boring jobs that employees dislike can also improve morale and interest as they take on increasingly more meaningful work. Accenture's Operations group, which has more than 100,000 employees, initially calculated that automation would replace 17,000 jobs in their accounts payable and marketing operations. However, headcount actually grew as employees moved to more strategic advisory services that expanded their business lines.[52]

The internet and mobile technology revolutions have created far more jobs than they have destroyed. AI will likely have the same effect, but new opportunities in the digital economy will require superior technical skills and knowledge. Demonstrating your commitment to retrain your employees for changing roles and responsibilities will go a long way toward gaining their consent and trust.

Educate Your Stakeholders

How would you react if you found out that your CEO doesn't know how to use a mobile phone, insists on handwritten correspondence, and has never heard of the internet? You can't expect your C-Suite to be experts in AI, but you can ensure that leading executives have a baseline education about machine intelligence.

When we train executives in the intricacies of AI, our curriculum is divided into an introductory module on our Machine Intelligence Continuum (MIC) framework and AI applications within a specific industry, a training module on how to evaluate an organization for AI-readiness, and a hands-on project to design and implement a pilot. Keep in mind that your executives will not need to know about the finer technical differences between algorithms. Your overall goal should be to teach your executives to gain a practical appreciation of what AI can do for your company. You'll want to include a theoretical introduction to help them separate hype from reality and also hands-on experience to help them understand both the limitations and potential of AI implementations in a corporate setting.

To learn more about our executive education offerings, visit **appliedaibook.com/education**.

7. INVEST IN TECHNICAL TALENT

Now that your company leaders and key stakeholders are both on board, the next challenge is to find people who have the necessary technical skills to staff your initiative. Finding the right people can be no less of a challenge than wrangling internal political support. Jean-François Gagné, founder of leading AI company Element.AI, calculated that there are fewer than 10,000 people in the world currently qualified to do state-of-the-art AI research and engineering.[53] Most of them are gainfully employed and hard to poach. If you're looking to recruit fresh graduates, the head of a prominent Silicon Valley AI lab recently confided to us that American universities only graduate about 100 competent researchers and engineers in this field each year!

The high demand for specialized AI talent, coupled with the painfully low supply, means that companies need to adopt new strategies when recruiting for a new AI initiative. Wealthier firms can afford to throw money at the problem by acqui-hiring AI startups at one to five million dollars per engineer.[54] Based on a study of public job listings among US employers, *Forbes* found that the top

20 AI recruiters, led by Amazon, Google, and Microsoft, spend more than $650 million annually to woo elusive researchers and engineers.[55]

What should you do if you don't have the deep pockets to go head-to-head against the Googles and Amazons of the world? Whether you're a new startup or an established enterprise looking to expand an AI project team, the following tips may help your company stand out in the noisy and competitive AI job market.

Understand Different Job Titles

Many companies struggle just to understand what "artificial intelligence" is, much less the myriad of titles, roles, skills, and technologies used to describe a prospective hire. Titles and descriptions vary from company to company, and terms are not well-standardized in the industry. However, most of the roles you encounter will resemble the following:

Data Science Team Manager
A data science team manager understands how best to deploy the expertise of his team in order to maximize their productivity on a project. This manager should have sufficient technical knowledge to understand what his team members are doing and how best to support them; at the same time, this manager must also have good communications skills in order to liaise with the leadership

or non-technical units. Though a person originally hired for a more junior role might organically fill this leadership position, teams that do not have designated and experienced managers are generally less productive.

Machine Learning (ML) Engineers

As their title indicates, ML engineers build machine learning solutions to solve business and customer problems. These specialized engineers deploy models, manage infrastructure, and run operations related to machine learning projects. They are assisted by data scientists and data engineers to manage databases and build the data infrastructure necessary to support the products and services used by their customers.

Data Scientists

Data scientists typically work in an offline setting and do not deal directly with the production experience, which is what the end user would see. Data scientists collect data, spend most of their time cleaning it, and the rest of their time looking for patterns in the data and building predictive models. They often have degrees in statistics, data science, or a related discipline. Alternately, many have programming backgrounds and hold degrees in computer science, math, or physics.

Researchers, Research Scientists

Researchers are more focused on driving scientific discovery and less concerned with pursuing industrial applications of their findings. They often build on promising leads uncovered by data scientists and experiment with novel approaches, much of which originates from or is inspired by work done in academic or industry research facilities.

Applied Research Scientists, Applied Research Engineers

Applied researchers straddle research and engineering. Unlike pure researchers, they are more concerned with practical research, such as identifying and implementing workable solutions to a specific problem or formulating industrial applications for scientific discoveries.

Data Engineers, Distributed Systems Engineers

Given the vast amounts of data and computation power required, most ML models face scalability issues. A talented infrastructure engineer can resolve challenges associated with large datasets, allowing researchers and data scientists to focus on their models rather than on data issues. Though this role is not explicitly focused on machine learning, it's a vital component of a complete ML team.

The composition of a machine learning team will change in response to the nature and timing of the project. Projects in fundamental research require more data and research scientists, whereas projects closer to production will require more applied researchers and infrastructure engineers.

Due to the limited talent pool, many enterprises may not

be able to hire applicants to fill all of these roles in-house. In this case, these companies could potentially fill in the gaps with enterprise solutions like Machine Learning as a Service (MLaaS) or AutoML technologies.

Seek the Right Characteristics

The skills required for successful careers in machine learning are different from those in traditional software development. Software development often has clearly structured tasks with well-defined deadlines for delivery and release. Once a key feature is done, engineers typically disengage and move on to another development project. While bug fixes and operational maintenance are required after completion, successful software development projects start with relatively clear specifications and product design and are launched when they meet release requirements.

By contrast, machine learning is highly exploratory and experimental, with less clear timelines and success metrics. Ideal performance targets may not be knowable in advance and may shift during a project. Algorithms require ongoing support, training, and feedback in order to perform optimally.

Mathematical Aptitude
A background in mathematics and statistics is far more valued in machine learning than in traditional software

engineering. Training ML models requires a sufficient background to understand which algorithms to apply and how to interpret and improve upon the results. For cutting-edge AI research positions, advanced mathematical intuition is a prerequisite in order to design and develop novel methodologies.

Curiosity

Training ML algorithms requires a constant sense of curiosity. The model builder needs to take in abstract information and make sense of it through continuous experimentation. This person will need to enjoy constantly learning new information and taking on new challenges.

Creativity

As ML tools and methodologies are still relatively new, the ability to think through ideas and to come up with novel ways to tackle a problem is highly valued. There will inevitably be many challenges that require new perspectives and solutions.

Perseverance

Artificial intelligence research is an ever-evolving pursuit. There are few simple answers, and it may easily take months to successfully train a viable algorithm. A successful individual will continue to try new techniques in the face of repeated failures until a solution can be found.

Rapid Learning

AI is evolving rapidly and keeping up-to-date with

the accomplishments in the field is critical. Successful candidates should be able to stay on top of the latest technical developments and to quickly and intelligently apply what they have learned.

Passion for Your Problem

"We get plenty of resumes from people with talented machine learning and data science backgrounds," says Zhen Jiang, Lead Analytics Supervisor at Ford Motor Company. "What I am much more concerned about is whether they have a passion for cars and mobility."[56] Talented engineers and researchers can go to any company in any industry that they want. Focus on finding applicants who are particularly excited by the unique problems that you face and the datasets that you own. Check whether they have done past research or projects related to your industry, and seek out talent at topical events that attract both enthusiasts and a more focused audience.

Knowing When to Stop

Perfect is the enemy of the good. Look for pragmatic applicants who recognize that a "good enough" model that meets product deadlines is better than a model that sits in development awaiting "just a few more tweaks." This quality can be hard to find, as most scientists and machine learning experts, especially those with PhDs, are often trained to seek perfection.

Optimize Recruiting Strategies

There is no one-size-fits-all hiring strategy for technical talent. When recruiting, be sure to tailor your approach to the level, background, and career goals of your prospects in order to maximize your chance of success.

JUNIOR ENGINEERS

Given the high interest in AI, machine learning, and data science, many universities offer competitive degree programs and graduate promising students every year. What junior engineers lack in experience, they often make up for in their willingness to learn and excel in their first few jobs out of school. However, sparse resumes can make it challenging for you to find the perfect match. Here's how we recommend overcoming these issues.

Cast a Wide Net

When hiring junior-level engineers, the prevailing strategy is to recruit widely. Since junior hires don't have the background or experience you can compare against a checklist of desired attributes, look for adaptive learners with a commitment to tackling hard challenges. Good candidates should have an interest in your industry and be excited to learn from more senior engineers.

Exploit University Partnerships

The preference for young and ambitious learners makes university partnerships another powerful means of recruitment. You can pitch ideas for and sponsor student projects. This mutually beneficial scenario allows you to identify top emerging talent and lets participating students get work experience in machine learning, creating a pipeline from academia to your business. SnapLogic, a software company headquartered in San Mateo, California, sponsors projects at the University of San Francisco (USF) where successful students can progress to paid internships and eventual employment after graduation. These partnership programs have become so popular that there are more companies proposing projects than students ready to staff them. Companies thinking about going this route should propose unique projects and clearly articulate the benefits of participation to attract the best students.

Host a "Hackathon"
A hackathon is a timeboxed event where people with technical backgrounds come together, form teams around a problem or idea, and collaboratively code a solution from scratch. Hackathons are increasingly being used to identify top coding talent and quick-thinking creatives.

Recruit from Specialized Training Programs
To meet the rising demand for machine learning talent, education programs have emerged to train junior talent and help them find job placements. Abhi Jha, Director of Advanced Analytics at McKesson, initially hired data science students from Galvanize, a technical skills training provider. "We've had a lot of success hiring

from career fairs that Galvanize organizes, where we present the unique challenges our company tackles in healthcare," he adds.[57]

EXPERIENCED SCIENTISTS AND RESEARCHERS

Hiring experienced data scientists and machine learning researchers requires a different approach. For these positions, employers typically look for a doctorate or extensive experience in machine learning, statistical modeling, or related fields. You will usually source these talented recruits through strategic networking, academic conferences, or blatant poaching. To this end, you can partner with universities or research departments and sponsor conferences to build your brand reputation.

You can also host competitions on Kaggle or similar platforms. Provide a problem, a dataset, and a prize purse to attract competitors. This is a good way to get international talent to work on your problem and will also build your reputation as a company that supports AI.

As with any industry, like attracts like. Dominant tech companies build strong AI departments by hiring superstar leaders. Google and Facebook attracted university professors and AI research pioneers such as Geoffrey Hinton, Fei-Fei Li, and Yann LeCun with plum appointments and endless resources. These professors either take a sabbatical from their universities or split their time between academia and industry.

EFFECTIVE ALTERNATIVES TO HIRING

Despite your best efforts, hiring new AI talent may prove to be slow or impossible. Be open minded about alternative ways to staff your technical initiatives.

Retrain Existing Engineers

Instead of going on the hunt for new talent, you can retrain current employees to fit your company's needs. While existing engineers may lack AI and machine learning knowledge, they will make up for it in loyalty and institutional knowledge.

Larger technology firms typically offer corporate training programs. Both Google and Facebook offer highly-competitive internal programs to retrain existing employees in machine learning and other AI techniques. Smaller firms can bring in external trainers. Alternatively, companies can provide employees paid access to extended education courses offered by online platforms, such as Coursera and Udacity, or by local universities. Apprenticeships are another way for engineers to add to their existing skill sets. Mentoring programs with more senior engineers or with data scientists can lead to fruitful partnerships.

Find Third-Party Solutions

The process of building an in-house machine learning product is likely to be onerous and slow, even for recognized brands. To meet business needs in the short-term, consider evaluating third-party solutions built by vendors who specialize in applying AI to enterprise functions.[58] Both startups and established enterprise vendors offer solutions to address common pain points for all departments, including sales and marketing, finance, operations and back-office, customer support, and even HR and recruiting.

Emphasize Your Company's Unique Advantages

At the end of an interview cycle, a strong AI candidate will have multiple offers in hand. In order to close the candidate, you'll need to differentiate your company from others. In addition to compensation, culture, and other general fit criteria, AI talent tends to evaluate offers on the following areas:

Availability of Data

Candidates want to be able to train their models with as much data as possible. The data should go back many years, if possible, and be real rather than inferred data.

Quality of Data

The data that you have for analysis is ideally clean and annotated. In a recent survey of data scientists, 57 percent reported that data cleaning consumed 60 percent of their time and was the least enjoyable part of their job.[59]

Diversity of Problems

Companies with smaller data stores can appeal to an applicant's intellectual curiosity by offering multiple challenges to solve.

Quality of the Team

Top talent wants to work with top talent. Offering junior candidates the opportunity to work with established experts or offering experts the best and brightest of the new recruits will appeal to both parties.

Impact of Work

Candidates want to know that their work will have meaningful impact and contribute to business success in a reasonable timeframe. Small companies that move quickly from idea conception to production can more quickly demonstrate the impact of their work. Larger companies with millions of customers can advertise the potential number of people that an algorithm can affect.

8. PLAN YOUR IMPLEMENTATION

Once you have assessed that your organization has the requisite culture, leadership, and talent to succeed in AI initiatives, the next step is to identify business opportunities with the highest return on investment (ROI).

Rank Business Goals

Prior to beginning any technology investment, you and your executive team must be clear on the problems you want to tackle, the reasons why solving these problems is a priority for your organization, and the metrics for success. You should have clear strategic goals at either the company- or department-level. Common goals include increasing revenue, cutting costs, and entering new business lines. Artificial intelligence can advance many of these goals, but implementation difficulty and impact will vary.

In the following sections, we give you several frameworks for evaluating current enterprise workflows and technologies, performing opportunity analysis, and clarifying your organizational goals and metrics.

Perform Opportunity Analysis

There are many analytical frameworks that you can use to discover where you should focus your AI investments. Common frameworks include Gap Analysis and SWOT.

GAP ANALYSIS

Gap analysis is used to assess where your business is versus where you would like it to be. The methodology relies on benchmarking, critical analysis, and action planning.

Goal and Objectives Setting

The first step to performing a gap analysis is to create clear goals. The objectives that you select can vary between companies, organizations, products, processes, etc. The key is to articulate useful goals that have clear objectives with appropriate, well-defined metrics for success.

Benchmarking

Benchmarking helps you to understand where you are and where you want to be. If you want to assess whether automation is worthwhile, you may want to compare your current performance with the performance of organizations that have already implemented automation. If it's difficult to get department-level metrics for competitors, consider hiring experts who have worked extensively with many companies to help you establish benchmarks. Don't limit yourself to data from your own industry. Technology companies have disrupted many traditional business models, so look beyond the obvious comparisons.

Gap Identification

After formulating goals and benchmarking your current performance against others, list all of the features associated with each objective that you want to achieve. Further break down those goals into their constituent parts. Compare where you are against where you want to be and identify the gaps between your current situation and your goals. Where are the biggest gaps? Complete this step for each goal that you are analyzing.

Action Planning

Once gaps have been identified, create a plan of action to address deficient areas.

What steps will you need to take to achieve them? How can you use automation to close this gap? The next step is to create a project plan that identifies how to fill those gaps. You can use a SWOT Analysis approach or our AI Strategy Framework, described in the next section, to hone in on opportunities.

SWOT ANALYSIS

SWOT stands for Strengths, Weaknesses, Opportunities, and Threats. This popular business framework can also be used to evaluate AI opportunities. Use this approach to uncover opportunities as well as potential weaknesses that you need to mitigate. You can apply the analysis to your own company as well as to competitors.

In a SWOT analysis, first evaluate the internal factors affecting your business. What are your strengths? What makes the department so great? Which projects or teams are finding success? Next consider your business's weaknesses. Which projects or departments are unprofitable? What resources do you lack? What can be done better?

The second half of a SWOT analysis considers the external factors, such as opportunities and threats, in the marketplace. What are your business goals? How can new technologies such as AI drive your enterprise forward? Are there new audiences that you should target? Finally, list any threats that may derail your company, department, or project. What obstacles do you face? Who is your primary competitor? Can you do anything to prevent or minimize potential threats?

AI Strategy Framework

How do you decide which problems to tackle first with AI? Our exclusive AI Strategy Framework provides a common set of criteria for evaluating each opportunity. The weighting of each factor will change depending on your business priorities.

First, understand the project's **strategic rationale**. How does the opportunity fit into your company or department's overall goals and strategic plan? Decide whether this is a revenue-increasing or a cost-cutting measure. How might this change the products and services that your company offers? Will it open new business opportunities? Typically, opportunities are judged against a mid- to long-term time horizon.

Next, consider the **opportunity size**. Is the opportunity big enough to warrant an AI solution, or can your employees or an older technology adequately solve the problem? Conversely, even if this specific opportunity can be solved more cheaply or easily with human power for now, can an AI-based solution be leveraged for similar tasks in the future?

Then, consider the **investment level** required. How much time and money will you need to allocate towards the problem? Don't forget to include internal costs. For example, even if an external vendor implements a solution, you will still incur internal management costs.

While the next factor, the **return on investment (ROI)**, is never certain, you should estimate an upper and lower bound and a likelihood of success. Understand your break-even number. Don't forget to include internal costs for project management and opportunity costs in your evaluation.

The fifth factor to consider is **risk**. What is the likelihood that this project will succeed and deliver on the projected ROI? Does this project seem like a sure bet, or is it a moonshot opportunity? Set the performance level that a new technology needs to achieve in order to be deemed successful. Also consider the industry risk of your competitors adopting AI for a core function. Would you lose your competitive advantage if you failed to take action?

Timeline is the next factor to consider. Most AI projects require at least a few months of investment before producing positive results for your business. During this period of time, you should constantly be optimizing and testing your technology. A project that will take years to complete should set interim milestones to measure progress.

Finally, have other business **stakeholders bought in**? Most projects will require an interdepartmental effort to gather data, train systems, launch new products, and maintain performance.

We've developed a more in-depth guide to our AI Strategy Framework that breaks down each of these major efforts into component steps, as well as checklists and recommendations to help you successfully apply our framework to your business. This premium resource is included with our executive education services, which you can learn more about at **appliedaibook.com/resources**.

Know Your Data and Analytics

Companies that have insufficient knowledge to answer questions about business opportunities and impact of AI, such as those in the early stages of developing an enterprise-wide data and analytics practice, may struggle with confidently ranking business goals via the AI Strategy Framework. As we explained in Chapter 6, "Building an AI-Ready Culture," an analytical culture is required to succeed in AI initiatives since accurate, centralized data is the foundation for developing effective machine learning solutions.

In such cases, you may need to take a step back and concentrate on earlier, more foundational aspects of building an enterprise-wide data practice. According to Michael Li, Head of Analytics and Data Science at LinkedIn, an organization can have five levels of analytics sophistication:[60]

Data: What Happened?

At this level, organizations want to use descriptive and exploratory statistics to answer fundamental business questions about what has happened in the past. This requires you to have collected the right kinds of data. In practice, we have found that while many enterprises have collected plenty of data, it is often dispersed across departments and owners, in the wrong format for analysis, or simply insufficient for answering basic business questions. If this applies to the use cases for which you're exploring AI and automation, you need to more clearly define your needs with requisite stakeholders in order to arrange for the correct data to be collected. Since knowing what has really happened in your business is critical for developing the best strategy for your future, this step is worth the investment of time, manpower, and budget.

Information and Knowledge: Why Did It Happen?

Once you and your executives are clear on what has happened in your business in the past, the next step is to understand why. During this phase, you move beyond statistical analysis of data into understanding and encoding expert logic for why certain results occurred. For example, your data may show that you had an unusually poor sales quarter last year. When analyzing your sales results along with data from human resources, you may discover that the poor showing is due to your top sales representatives leaving the company around that time. While some knowledge can be encoded, others will require you to augment your quantitative analysis with qualitative interviews and external research.

Intelligence: What Will Happen?

All businesses want to make key predictions, such as whether a prospect will become a paying customer or if an existing customer is in danger of churning. Machine learning and AI approaches can be used to deliver accurate and effective results only when your company has demonstrated mastery of the previous two levels. If you lack the requisite data, then you're missing information about your business that is critical to your high-level strategy. If you have data but not the domain expertise to interpret that data, you are at risk of feeding the wrong assumptions into your intelligent systems, which will invariably produce the wrong results.

Insights: What's the Best That Could Happen?

Machine learning can also be used to discover opportunities you weren't aware of, such as new customer segments you can target, more effective messaging and processes for your sales and marketing functions, or a superior product design that improves retention. While predictive AI systems are usually built on past data, you can also employ AI solutions to generate new ideas and conduct large-scale experiments to test and evaluate new ideas rapidly.

Change and Impact: How Can We Automate Continuous Transformation?

The ultimate outcome for an analytics practice is to tighten and automate the feedback loop between data, insights, action, and results. For example, the goal of just-in-time manufacturing is to dynamically adjust factory output based on real-time consumer demand data from retail and digital touchpoints. For companies producing digital mobile and web experiences, the user experience and user interface (UX/UI) can be automatically optimized based on a specific user profile and browsing behavior.

Achieving this idealistic goal across industries and functions requires more than just technological sophistication and tools that can automatically recommend, execute, and monitor actionable insights. You will also need a fast-moving and tech-savvy workforce that has mastered analytical decision-making, change management, AI systems development, and leadership skills for managing autonomous organizations.

Technical Prerequisites

Artificial intelligence techniques are most economically used to automate problems that are time-consuming, repetitive, and simple in scope. Most machine learning approaches also require large quantities of clean, trainable data. Just because a problem can be automated does not mean that an AI solution is appropriate. For example, using AI to generate an annual shareholder report may not be a good investment if you can easily hire analysts to do the work more cheaply than you can build or buy a software alternative. The task also requires strategic communication and contextual understanding, which modern AI technologies struggle with. By contrast, automating the sales process provides faster service to your customers and reduces the likelihood of clerical error, which can create value by streamlining paperwork, improving record keeping, and increasing cash flow.

Here are key questions to ask when evaluating whether your problem needs an AI solution:

1. **Is this a process that can be solved using machine learning?** Break down the process into its components to determine inputs, outputs, and contingencies. How long does it take to perform? How often is each step taken? How many people perform the same task? This gives a sense of the opportunity size for automation.

2. **Is it suitable for machine learning?** Identify the decision-making process for each task component. Do answers to questions come to you immediately, or do they require longer deliberation? Furthermore, if multiple people were answering the same question, would they all reach the same conclusion? Machine learning is best used to replicate human decisions for tasks where correct answers are clear and measurable.

3. **Is data available?** Are there sufficient volumes of relevant data associated with the process

from which an algorithm can learn? How easily accessible is the data? Do you have a technical team that can manage and analyze the data? How long will they need to transform the data into a usable format?

If you answered in the affirmative to all three questions, your project may be suitable for AI.

Build vs. Buy

If you ask your engineers whether you should build your own machine learning software, they will almost always say yes. What technologist doesn't want to master the latest and greatest innovations and play with shiny new tools? Unfortunately, this is rarely the correct solution for most companies, especially those that are still completing digital transformations and have not repeatedly demonstrated the ability to design, develop, and ship successful technology to both internal and external customers.

Many of the tech giants offer to "democratize AI" by releasing open-source development tools such as Keras, TensorFlow, CTNK, and PyTorch, or offer enterprise cloud solutions and proprietary Machine Learning as a Service (MLaaS) platforms. For companies that don't have the infrastructure or the technical knowledge, these represent excellent solutions for quickly integrating AI capabilities

into your company's workflow . If you already store data
and build applications on Amazon Web Services (AWS),
Microsoft Azure, Google Cloud, or Apple's iOS platform,
using tightly integrated machine learning solutions like
AWS Rekognition or Apple's Core ML can simplify work
for your own developers and may be the most economical
business decision.

However, the mere existence of a solution does not mean
that it's definitely right for your company. In the digital
era, data is the hottest commodity. Many executives tell
us that they are concerned with the potential business
impact of sharing data and outsourcing technical
expertise. Google, Amazon, Facebook, and other internet
giants already own an enormous amount of data about
your customers and employees. These tech companies
often know more than you do about what your customers
search for, what they buy, what they say, who they interact
with, where they are, and how they might behave in the
future. Their expertise has helped them to grow rapidly
with high profit margins, overwhelming less tech-savvy
competitors in the process.

Technology companies may not compete directly
with you today, but heed prominent venture capitalist
Marc Andreessen's warning that "software is eating
the world."[61] As consumers opt for the convenience of
Amazon Prime and investors question other companies'
abilities to compete against the "Amazon Effect," retailers
across a wide range of industries have seen their profits

and stock values decline.[62] Amazon has even launched private labels for popular product categories that directly compete for market share with third-party sellers on their own platform.[63] Web traffic and advertising revenues have plummeted at many online media publishers.[64] Even though digital advertising spending is growing, Google and Facebook present a duopoly that captured 85 percent of the new growth in the first quarter of 2016.[65]

Technological superiority alone cannot account for success. Even well-funded tech behemoths have failed when entering new markets or when copying the products of their competitors because they failed to master business fundamentals first. However, as data, analytics, automation, and AI have infiltrated all aspects of modern life, companies primed to take advantage of them will have no problem trouncing those that are unprepared.

Should you invest in your technical capabilities and turn your organization into a technology company like Google and Amazon? Or should you stick to your core business expertise and find third-party solutions for your AI needs? Here are some criteria that will guide your decision-making process:

BUILDING INTERNALLY

There are several important criteria to consider when thinking about building in-house.

First, determine whether your technology is a **core functionality** of your business. In 2001, Target outsourced its e-commerce website to Amazon because the company executives did not see online shopping as a major revenue channel. Nearly a decade later, Target finalized realized that this was a huge mistake and took back control.[66] As a leader, you will have to judge whether the AI capability that you want to build is central to your long-term business.

Second, evaluate the **availability of in-house talent**. There is a massive skills shortage in the field of artificial intelligence. Even if your organization has a sufficient pool of talent for core products and services, you may hesitate to deploy these scarce resources to departments such as HR or customer service. The need for technical talent extends beyond the initial build, as you'll need specialists for ongoing maintenance and performance monitoring.

Third, set a **timeline for deployment**. Even if your company has the talent and the data to build a custom solution, you may not have access to them until higher-priority projects have been addressed. In many instances, your fastest solution may be a proof-of-concept with an external vendor.

Fourth, assess the **availability of data** for your project. Having tons of data doesn't mean that you have the right data. Even medium to large enterprises often don't have enough of the right data to train a machine learning algorithm in-house to an acceptable performance level. In comparison, a solution provider with numerous clients may have access to millions of aggregated customer inquiries. Using a third-party platform that has clients in the same industry can also give your organization the benefits of knowledge transfer and additional domain expertise.

Finally, **total ownership cost** is a key factor when deciding whether to build or buy. If you decide to build, how much will it cost in internal resources? Be sure to include ongoing maintenance and upgrade costs. If you decide to buy, how much will it cost in the long run? If usage volume will increase, factor in how that may affect pricing. Many organizations estimate that 70 percent of their IT department budget is spent on maintaining existing infrastructure rather than to develop new projects.[67] Conduct an honest lifecycle analysis of the estimated costs of continual in-house maintenance versus that of external licensing.

EVALUATING VENDORS

Given the hype, many third-party vendors claim to "use AI" but are really using the phrase as a marketing tool. When looking at our Machine Intelligence Continuum from Chapter 2, you'll see that most vendors are actually using technologies that fall under Systems That Act and Systems That Predict, *not* Systems That Learn. To differentiate between value and hype, be sure to probe any prospective solution provider on the following:

Access to Data

Many companies are developing machine learning algorithms, but those with access to large volumes of proprietary data have an advantage. Likewise, those that can leverage their proprietary methods to extract maximum value from smaller but more relevant data stores can also excel. Look for partners with access to a lot of data that's relevant to your domain.

Domain Specificity

Companies with many clients in the same industry can leverage their knowledge across customers. An AI-based customer-support solution for e-commerce will already know how to process common questions such as "Where is my order?" and "How do I return a product?" Greater domain knowledge in a field allows for faster integration at lower cost. Furthermore, these providers are more likely to include features relevant to your business on their product roadmaps.

Team Talent

AI is a growth industry facing a massive skills shortage. When you evaluate a provider, look at the backgrounds and qualifications of the founders, key engineers, and product teams on their website or LinkedIn page. Most importantly, ask yourself if they truly understand your business and your problems. You want the right solution, not just a fancy one. Avoid AI startups that operate like hammers looking for nails, assuming any and all enterprise challenges can be solved with machine learning. Worry about the vendor's technical pedigree only after confirming whether its proposed solution is a match for your business needs.

ROI Metrics

When choosing between potential partners, evaluate how they measure successful outcomes. Are their reporting metrics aligned with yours? Transparency in reporting suggests that a company has faith in its product and experience working with customers similar to you.

Client Experience

Evaluate a company's expertise by examining its client list. In particular, look for specific and tangible results from customer case studies that resemble your use cases. When a company provides references freely or offers a risk-free evaluation process, it is demonstrating confidence in its product and customer experience.

Ease of Integration

Solution providers will quote integration timelines that range from a few days to a few months. Understand what's involved in their implementation process and their timeline for completion. What kind of support will they provide? Who is responsible for the data and technical integration? When should you expect to see results? Integration may also depend heavily on your organizational readiness. Be honest and ask prospective providers about what they will need from you and your team.

Pricing

Find a company that has a pricing model aligned with your business goals. Can you readily demonstrate the ROI to your CFO or CEO using their pricing information? Does the model account for your growth and future needs to deliver additional economic value over time? Does it include costs for maintenance and ongoing optimizations?

Security

With cybersecurity breaches at the forefront of the news these days, it's essential that your technology partner addresses security issues. Can the product meet the governmental, regulatory, and industry-specific compliance requirements? What is your partner's game plan for handling worst-case scenarios?

Data Connection

Does the prospective product offer seamless connections with the other enterprise tools on which you depend, such as your data and analytics provider or CRM system? Is the integration built-in, and if so, is it offered via an application programming interface (API) or platform? If not, will it require custom development?

Language Support

If you're working on a consumer-facing global product, such as a conversational agent or sentiment analysis, your solution may need to support additional languages. How many languages and types of voices does the prospective product support?

Professional Support

Most AI systems will need to be continually trained and updated. How accessible and competent is the vendor's professional services team to help onboard and maintain your AI system? Particularly for large enterprises, does the vendor have the capability to support the scale of service that you require?

Regulatory Requirements

Legislation may require your business to explain critical technology decisions. Many government regulations apply levels of control on the use of consumer data and software algorithms in certain contexts. For example, the FDA regulates the use of machine learning models in health care. In Europe, the General Data Protection Regulation (GDPR) asserts sweeping authority to restrict "automated individual decision-making" in the evaluation of a person's "performance at work, economic situation, health, personal preferences, interests, reliability, behavior, location, or movements."[68] The GDPR also provides EU citizens with the "right to explanation," in which they have the option of reviewing the decision of a particular algorithm.[69] If your organization is subject to industry-specific or location-specific regulatory requirements, make sure that the AI system that you are using is not a black box and can comply with the required levels of transparency and reliability.

Limits of Use

No third-party solution will be perfect for your use case,

so it is equally important to understand the features as well as the limitations of the software that you decide to buy. The sales staff at a vendor company may not have enough incentive to be fully honest with you, so the best way to get honest answers is usually to survey their existing customers. Ask them if they have run into problems with scalability, stability, security, compatibility, or ease of use. What frustrates them most about the product? What do they wish it could do that it currently can't? Keep in mind that technologies and the companies behind them are constantly evolving, so also find out how quickly and robustly a company addresses reported issues and improves the performance of their solutions.

Competitive Landscape

How does a specific vendor stack up against competition in the same industry or vertical? Since AI is heavily dependent on data, vendors that are unable to capture a sufficient portion of the market may find themselves falling further and further behind the market leaders. This may negatively impact their ability to deliver an excellent product or service to you, their customer. We track and assess vendors that offer AI-powered products for enterprise functions in our Enterprise AI Landscape. To access this exclusive content, visit our book website at **appliedaibook.com/resources**.

Evaluating vendors can be a time-consuming and complex process, especially given the sales and marketing jargon that many of these AI companies use. In addition to our Enterprise AI Landscape, we offer a more detailed guide on how to evaluate enterprise AI solutions at **appliedaibook.com/resources**.

TRANSITIONING FROM BUILD TO ASSEMBLE TO BUY

Even if you have the necessary team, data, and time to build a complete AI solution in-house, it may not be strategic to invest so many resources upfront without proven ROI. In many cases, companies will start testing automation strategies by first buying from third-party vendors, then assembling a mix of external and internal technologies, and finally transitioning to a fully in-house and customized solution if necessary.

Many vendor solutions which purport to use AI are point solutions which address a single problem very well but can't support the complex workflows you need to do business. This is especially true in productivity software for sales and marketing. Thousands of vendors have flooded the market, but very few contain all the features that enterprise customers need. You'll often need to fill the gaps that are not addressed by the platform that you have bought.

Vendors may also be costly compared to in-house development, exhibit latency or unavailability if they are cloud-only solutions, or fail to meet your data security requirements. Many also optimize algorithms for specific tasks but do not help you optimize your end-to-end machine learning pipeline or your overall business workflow.

Building a fully customized, in-house solution means you can build an end-to-end system that addresses all required aspects of your business workflow and technical integrations. You can optimize the entire pipeline, not just algorithms for specific tasks. You have a high degree of flexibility and can specialize in developing capabilities unique to your organization. Finally, you can design the exact security infrastructure you need to meet company and industry standards.

In transitioning from buy to build, an important consideration is whether there exists open-source software that will allow you to affordably customize and extend pre-built features without paying hefty costs to a third party. Open-source solutions exist for virtually all aspects of a machine learning platform, ranging from solutions that manage your data layer, model development and management, and higher-level analytics and reporting. Popular open-source solutions for building big data and AI platforms include Apache Hadoop and Spark, H2O.ai, Scikit-Learn, and TensorFlow. Such solutions can be mixed with paid enterprise solutions to achieve the functionality, scalability, stability, and security you require.

Calculate ROI and Allocate Budget

Impressive ROI on successful projects whets our appetites for AI. Through better search algorithms, Netflix reduced cancelled subscriptions that would have dropped revenue by one billion dollars annually.[70] Peloton, a popular indoor cycling company, cut customer support tickets by 25 percent with intelligent self-service.[71] Harley-Davidson used AI to target potential customers and to adjust their sales copy, increasing sales leads in New York by 2,930 percent.[72]

However, a 2017 McKinsey report found that 41 percent of businesses reported that the uncertain return on investments was one of the biggest barriers preventing them from adopting AI. Because the scope, ongoing maintenance costs, and maturity level of AI technologies vary widely, it is difficult to produce a generalized methodology to quantify ROI for AI.

An alternate measure may be to examine how AI technology unlocks business value. Typical metrics center around tangibles such as increased revenue and decreased costs, as well as intangibles such as culture, brand value, and work-life balance.

INCREASING REVENUE

First, you can assess its revenue creation ability, most

notably in external-facing departments such as sales, marketing, and customer service. AI can identify new potential customers for the sales team, facilitate personalization to improve conversion rates and decrease churn, and power customer service bots to provide higher quality service and generate repeat business. Read Chapters 17, 18, and 19 for more detailed analysis on popular AI applications for these business functions.

AI may also allow you to offer new products or services that weren't previously possible. Historically, customers engaged Deloitte to review procurement contracts in order to calculate precise merger and acquisition synergies after closing a deal. It was an expensive process that required a dozen people and four to five months to complete. Using natural language classification techniques, Deloitte slashed the time needed for review down to a week. The company now offers this as a service to companies for evaluating potential acquisition targets.[73]

To calculate revenue gains, make predictions on price changes and the volume of sales. Will the quality of your service increase substantially, and will that allow you to adjust your prices? The opportunity may not be large enough for the multiplier effect to be worth it. If you're operating off of a miniscule customer base, then even a 200 percent increase in a key metric may not lead to meaningful boosts to revenue. If the problem is worth pursuing, then how much can better conversion rates and longer lifetime values improve sales volume?

If you're partnering with a vendor, ask them for performance metrics. What results have other clients seen? What is the upper and lower limit of improvements? When did they begin to see results?

DECREASING COSTS

Measuring the ability to reduce costs is another popular way to assess returns on AI investments. AI promises greater operational efficiencies, predominantly in middle and back office functions, such as in legal, finance and accounting, operations, and human resources. However, efficiency alone is not valuable. Focus instead on the increased output or decreased human capital costs that are made possible by efficiency gains. Don't forget to include potential cost reductions that result from improved compliance and decreased legal risks. We cover additional details about how AI is used to improve internal business operations in Chapters 13, 14, and 15.

To calculate potential cost reductions, map out the current situation. Follow the operational procedure and note all of the steps that employees must perform as well as the number of employees needed for each task. How long do they need to finish each step? How many total man-hours are spent on the project? What is the fully-loaded cost of these full time equivalents (FTE)? How often is this process repeated?

Then, consider whether these employees can be retrained to perform higher-value and more lucrative work. Keep in mind that automation generally only eliminates a fraction of an employee's responsibilities, so be sure not to overestimate potential gains.

Third, consider the intangible benefits that you may reap. Investing in AI has been associated with improving corporate culture and encouraging innovation. Automation in the customer service sector has freed up human agents to focus on more interesting and complicated cases, leading to higher morale and lower turnover.[74] Investing in automation can also foster innovation and creative thinking as well as enhance productivity. If deployed wisely, automation will be welcomed, not feared, by your employees.

Finally, what is the opportunity cost of inaction? Your competitors will invest in AI capabilities even if you don't. They will leverage their capabilities to offer a better product at a lower price. By that time, you may not be able to catch up.

MEASURING ROI

Benchmarking human work gives us a baseline against which we can compare AI systems. Machine learning solutions do not need to be perfect to provide value. To be worth your investment, the technology may only need to perform at near-human levels. You can buy more computers and run them 24/7 more easily than you can hire, train, and manage staff to perform the same tasks. Machine learning systems will also improve over time with proper data management and fine-tuning.

The total time scale for calculating ROI for projects varies. Most AI projects should aim to break even within a few quarters, at most a year.[75] Specific estimates will depend on project complexity and whether you are building the solution in-house or using an external provider. Well-established providers can offer faster roll out times, leading to quicker ROI, with some solution providers even promising gains on the first day. Especially for pilots, you should see returns through cost reduction, risk mitigation, or revenue generation within a year, if not significantly sooner.

PORTFOLIO APPROACH

Consider taking a portfolio or a venture capitalist approach to evaluating returns on AI projects.[76] View these early investments as research and development (R&D) ventures and assume that lots of failures will accompany each success. Many of the projects with the biggest ROI also take the longest to mature, require the most investment, and involve the most risk. Therefore, select a variety of projects based on their respective investment requirements, expected time to results, and likelihood of success. Schedule the experiments across multiple quarters and intersperse sure wins with riskier projects. If you're restricted to testing one project at a time, prioritize likely wins in order to gain credibility and flexibility for future projects.

Pick the Right "True North" Metric

How can you tell if your AI strategy is creating long-term and sustainable value? Answering this question can be the most difficult and most impactful step of your machine learning process.

Even after you've ascertained that an AI initiative is likely to positively impact the bottom line of your business, you need to define a more specific "true north" metric for each major project in order to keep your machine learning projects on the right trajectory. Goals like "Increase revenue by X dollars" or "Cut costs by Y percent" are almost always too high-level to be useful, since a confluence of intermediate factors drive your end result. Choosing a more specific metric helps you to qualify your AI strategy and also check that your decisions align and advance your business and technology in the right direction.

Facebook's true north metric for platform growth is the number of members who connect with ten friends in seven days.[77] Just having a user sign up for an account is insufficient to inspire the engagement rates that Facebook needs to later monetize that user through advertising.

Similarly, Slack focuses on teams that have exchanged at least 2,000 messages.[78] Once a team has reached this threshold of usage, they're much more likely to stick around and eventually upgrade to paid plans.

Identifying the right true north metric can be a challenge. Ask yourself the following questions to avoid the common mistakes executives make.

Is this a metric everyone can understand? Avoid using jargon or overly technical terminology when defining your true north metric. You want to align your entire company, not just a handful of domain experts, to your AI strategy goals. Optimize for simplicity, transparency, and ease of communication.

Is this a vanity or a success metric? You may have tons of page views, but those aren't useful unless you are also converting those visitors into more paying customers. Be sure your true north metric is an accurate proxy for success.

Is this a leading or a lagging indicator? Lagging indicators like post-purchase behavior may be useful for evaluating the condition of your business but they may come too late to inform your daily business decisions.

Is this a relative or absolute metric? Absolute metrics such as the total number of registered users will always increase. Don't fall into the trap of using such metrics to stroke your ego. A relative metric such as the number of monthly active users (MAU) can be used to compute a rate of change for comparative analysis between different periods.

Is this metric actionable? Do you know what you will do if you don't hit your minimum thresholds for your true north metrics? What about when your performance exceeds expectations? An effective metric needs to help you filter out unproductive follow-up actions and prioritize impactful ones.

Is the metric tracked and measured correctly? Adjustments almost always need to be made to correctly compare results from different periods. For example, you may need to account for seasonality or remove statistical anomalies such as outliers. You'll also need to perform a sanity check to make sure that the data sources used to compute your metric are free of bias and mistakes.

Is our true north metric really aligned with our business goals? The right true north metric may not be immediately obvious. Companies may need to experiment a little before honing in on the right metric. You're likely to generate new insights during every round of experimentation which will help you realize what actually drives business results. Once you have confidence that a metric is productive, however, it's best to stay consistent until you have strong reasons to optimize for a new goal.

Constantly switching true north metrics will confuse your team and hinder your execution.

9. COLLECT AND PREPARE DATA

In Chapter 4, we discussed examples of harmful outcomes that may result when AI models rely on unreliable, biased, or incomplete data. The lessons of that chapter are important enough to bear repeating: *data is not reality*.

Data Is Not Reality

Data is a human invention. Humans define the phenomenon that they want to measure, design systems to collect data about it, clean and pre-process it before analysis, and finally choose how to interpret the results. Even with the same dataset, two people can form vastly different conclusions. This is because data alone is not "ground truth," which is defined by machine learning experts as observable, provable, and objective data that reflects reality. If data was inferred from other information, relies on subjective judgment, collected in a slipshod manner, or is of questionable authenticity, then it is not ground truth.

How you choose to conceptualize a phenomenon, determine what to measure, and decide how to take measurements will all impact the data that you collect. Your ability to solve a problem with artificial intelligence depends heavily on how you frame your problem and also whether you can establish ground truth without ambiguity. Ground truth is used as a benchmark to assess the performance of algorithms. If your gold standard is wrong, then your results will not only be wrong but also potentially harmful to your business.

Unless you were directly involved with defining and monitoring your original data collection goals, instruments, and strategy, you are likely missing critical knowledge that may result in incorrect processing, interpretation, and use of that data.

Common Mistakes With Data

What people call "data" can be carefully curated measurements selected purely to support an agenda, haphazard collections of random information with no correspondence to reality, or information that looks reasonable but resulted from unconsciously biased collection efforts. Here's a crash course on statistical errors with which every executive should be familiar.

UNDEFINED GOALS

Failing to pin down the reason for collecting data means that you'll miss the opportunity to articulate assumptions and to determine what to collect. The result is that you'll likely collect the wrong data or incomplete data. A common trend in big data is for enterprises to gather heaps of information without any understanding of why they need it and how they want to use it. Gathering huge but messy volumes of data will only impede your future analytics, since you'll have to wade through much more irrelevant junk to find what you actually want.

DEFINITION ERROR

Let's say you want to know how much your customers spent on your products last quarter. Seems like an easy task, right? Unfortunately, even a simple goal like this will require fleshing out a number of assumptions before you can get the information that you want.

First, how are you defining "customer"? Depending on your goals, you might not want to lump everyone into one bucket. You may want to segment customers by their purchasing behavior in order to adjust your marketing efforts or product features more effectively. If that's the case, then you'll need to be sure that you're including useful information about the customer, such as demographic information or spending history.

There are also logistical considerations, such as deciding how to define a quarter. Will you use fiscal quarters or calendar quarters? Many organizations have fiscal years that do not correspond with calendar years. Fiscal years also differ internationally, with Australia's fiscal year starting on July 1st and India's fiscal year starting on April 1st.[79] You will also need a strategy to account for returns or exchanges. What if a customer bought your product in one quarter but returned it in another? What if they filed a quality complaint against you and received a refund? Do you net these in the last quarter or this one?

As you can see, definitions are not so simple. You will need to discuss your expectations and set appropriate parameters in order to collect the information that you actually want.

CAPTURE ERROR

Once you've identified the type of data that you wish to collect, you'll need to design a mechanism to capture it. Mistakes here can result in capturing incorrect or accidentally biased data. Let's say you want to test whether product A is more compelling than product B, but you always display product A first on your website. Because users do not see or purchase product B as frequently, the results of your test will lead you to the wrong conclusion.

MEASUREMENT ERROR

Measurement errors occur when the software or hardware that you use to capture data goes awry, either failing to capture usable data or producing spurious data. For example, information about user behavior on your mobile app may be lost if usage logs are not synchronized with your servers due to connectivity issues. Similarly, when you use a microphone, your audio recordings may capture background noise or interference from other electrical signals.

PROCESSING ERROR

As you can see from our simple attempt to calculate customer sales figures earlier, many errors can occur even before you look at your data. Many enterprises own data that is decades-old, and the original team capable of explaining important decisions surrounding data collection or data storage may be long gone. Many of their assumptions and issues are likely not documented and will be up to you to deduce, which can be a daunting task.

You and your team may achieve wildly different results by making assumptions that differ from the original ones made during data collection. Common errors include missing a particular filter that may have been used on the data, such as the removal of outliers; using different accounting standards, as in the case with financial reporting; and simply making calculation errors.

COVERAGE ERROR

Coverage error describes what happens with survey data when there is insufficient opportunity for all targeted respondents to participate. For example, if you are collecting data on the elderly but only offer a website survey, you'll probably miss out on many respondents.

In the case of digital products, your marketing teams may be interested in projecting how all mobile smartphone users might behave with a prospective product. However, if you only offer an iOS app and not an Android app, the iOS user data will give you limited insight into how Android users may behave.

SAMPLING ERROR

Sampling errors occur when you analyze data from a smaller sample that is not representative of your target population. This is unavoidable when data only exists for some groups within a population. The conclusions that you draw from the unrepresentative sample will probably not apply to the whole. Asking only your friends for opinions about your products and then assuming your user population will feel similarly is a classic sampling error.

INFERENCE ERROR

Inference errors are made by statistical or machine learning models when they make incorrect predictions from the available ground truth. Two types of inference errors can occur: false negatives and false positives. False positives occur when you incorrectly predict that an item belongs in a category when it does not, such as saying that a patient has cancer when he is healthy. False negatives occur when an item is in a category but you predict that it is not, such as when a patient with cancer is predicted to be cancer-free.

Assuming you have a clean record of ground truth, calculating inference errors will help you to assess the performance of your machine learning models. However, the reality is that many real-world datasets are noisy and may be mislabeled, which means that you may not have clarity on the exact inference errors that your AI system is making.

UNKNOWN ERROR

Reality can be elusive, and you cannot always establish ground truth with ease. In many cases, such as with digital products, you can capture tons of data about what a user did on your platform but not his motivation for those actions. You may know that a user clicked on an advertisement, but you don't know how annoyed she may have been with it.

In addition to many known types of errors, there are unknown unknowns about the universe that leave a gap between your representation of reality, in the form of data, and reality itself.

10. BUILD MACHINE LEARNING MODELS

Business leaders who want to lead AI initiatives at their companies should develop a high-level understanding of how machine learning models are built, even if you are not responsible for writing the code yourself. Your willingness to educate yourself on general technical details will improve your credibility and communication with the engineers on your team.

AI Is Not a Silver Bullet

Machine learning is a powerful tool, but it is not right for everything. As with any technology, some use cases will benefit more than others from the application of AI. Each algorithm has distinct advantages that make it more successful in some scenarios but not in others. AI experts and engineers are well-versed in these details, but most executives who lack technical backgrounds tend to clump all AI technologies together and regard it as a silver bullet.

If you haven't read our opening chapters on basic AI terminology and the Machine Intelligence Continuum, you should do so now. Even if you're familiar with technical concepts, you'll benefit from the definitions and conceptual framework that we present in those chapters for thinking about machine intelligence. We focus much of our book on machine learning and deep learning techniques since these algorithms are widely used in enterprise solutions. Many other approaches to AI exist and will be covered at our website, **appliedaibook.com**.

If you haven't done the exercises from the preceding chapters to help you identify and prioritize implementation opportunities in your business, make sure you do them before jumping to conclusions about which AI solutions you need. Don't be dazzled by shiny products that aren't relevant to your problems. We often see smart executives make technology investments that don't drive actual business profitability.

The foundation of artificial intelligence is data. Even perfectly-implemented algorithms will fail without the right data. This is no different from a human expert arriving at the wrong conclusions after being given the wrong facts. Many theoretical AI examples assume that you possess enough of the right kind of data, but in the real world, data is often irrelevant, incomplete, or messy. Review the discussion of common mistakes with data in Chapter 9 to avoid obvious pitfalls in your own data-gathering process.

Assessing the Performance of Your Models

You'll need evaluation metrics to assess the performance of any model or to compare the performance of competing models. In the previous chapter, we discussed different types of inference errors, including the false positive error and the false negative error. Accuracy, precision, and recall build on these concepts, and they are the most common evaluation metrics for classification tasks, in which a model evaluates some input as belonging or not belonging to a target category.

Actual Values

		True	False
Predicted Values	True	**True Positive** Correct Prediction	**False Positive** Incorrect Prediction
	False	**False Negative** Incorrect Prediction	**True Negative** Correct Prediction

Accuracy	Precision	Recall
True Positives + True Negatives	True Positives	True Positives
True Positives + True Negatives + False Positives + False Negatives	True Positives + False Positives	True Positives + False Negatives

Accuracy

Accuracy gives the percentage of classifications that were correctly made. For example, if you are building an email spam filter, the accuracy metric would tell you the number of messages that the filter correctly identified as being spam (true positive) or as being legitimate (true negative) out of all of the messages in your inbox.

A perfect model has an accuracy of 1, because it will have correctly classified everything. Be wary when you hear AI vendors or the media quote impressive accuracy numbers for a machine learning model. Accuracy alone typically does not provide enough information for you to evaluate a model's performance.

Precision

Precision measures the percentage of true outcomes that were correctly identified out of all of the true classifications that were made. To put it another way, precision tells us the model's ability to correctly classify the instances that we care about in a dataset.

Email spam filters perform a binary classification task, in

which it looks at a message and tries to determine whether it is spam (the target category) or not spam. These filters work well most of the time, but they occasionally make a wrong classification, which then either sends a spam message to your inbox or hides a legitimate message in your spam folder. Measuring the precision of a spam filter would tell you the number of messages that the filter correctly identifies as being spam (true positive) out of the total number of messages that it classified as spam, both actual spam messages (true positive) and legitimate messages that were mistakenly labeled (false positive).

Recall

Recall measures the percentage of true outcomes that were correctly classified as being true. In other words, recall characterizes a model's ability to identify all of the instances that we should care about in a dataset.[80]

Going back to the spam filter, the true outcomes are all of the spam messages that were received by your email account. However, because spam filters are imperfect, the recall metric would tell you the number of spam messages that were correctly identified as being spam and filtered out (true positive) out of the total number of spam messages, both correctly flagged (true positive) and incorrectly flagged (false negative), that were received.

Trade-offs

There's a trade-off between optimizing the precision and recall of a model. The nature of your task will determine whether it's more important to maximize precision, to maximize recall, or to achieve a balance between the two.

For use cases that are more innocuous, such as our spam filter example, you may want to optimize for precision because minimizing false positives is arguably better. False negatives such wacky solicitations from Nigerian princes that were mis-flagged as being innocuous, are a nuisance to your inbox, but you can deal with them quickly by hitting the delete button. By contrast, accidentally flagging an email from an important business partner as spam could result in lost opportunity and revenue for your business.

You will want to optimize for recall in use cases that carry more severe consequences, such as cancer diagnoses. Emphasizing recall minimizes false negatives, or cases in which a patient is actually sick but was misdiagnosed as being healthy. A false negative diagnosis would result in disastrous outcomes for a sick patient, while a false positive diagnosis would mostly inconvenience a healthy patient. Even if you end up with a few false positives, you will correctly identify the most number of patients who actually have cancer. Though both are undesirable, false negatives in this specific use case are worse.

Common Mistakes With Machine Learning Models

Bad data invariably leads to bad results. Even if you've taken care to eliminate errors from your training data, you can still make mistakes with your algorithms.

The ultimate goal of any predictive model is to make accurate predictions about unseen data. A good model should first extrapolate patterns from your training data to correctly predict outcomes with reasonable accuracy, then, it should be able to generalize, applying what it has learned to make reasonably accurate predictions on new data.

Selection of the correct data is critical to the success of your model. If the data that you select is unrelated to the model or is inherently random, then no amount of tweaking will improve your model's ability to generalize. However, even if your data fits the problem at hand, the ability of predictive models to generalize is still susceptible to two problems: underfitting and overfitting.

Underfitting

Underfitting occurs when your model is too simple to capture the complexities of your underlying data. Let's say that you want to sell your house, and you want to build a model to determine the appropriate market price by using data about other home sales in your neighborhood. If you tell the model to only consider the location of property and ignore other attributes, like square footage or included amenities, then its predictions won't reflect the true relationship between houses and their prices, even if you had given it an accurate dataset for training.

Overfitting

Overfitting occurs when your model does not generalize well outside of your training data. Let's say that new home buyers moving to your city really value proximity to organic, family-owned grocery stores, and your house happens to be right next to one. If you factor in distance from these specific stores into your pricing model, then you may be able to predict nearby home prices in your training data with extreme accuracy. However, your model will probably perform very poorly when trying to predict housing prices in other locations where buyer values differ.

Overcoming problems with underfitting and overfitting require careful examination of your data and understanding which aspects are most relevant to the problems you need to solve. These issues can also be mitigated by employing a rigorous validation and test process, which is described in the next section.

Machine Learning Workflow

Machine learning projects benefit from following a structured workflow, which starts with clearly defining business goals.

If you're unclear on what you actually want to achieve, do the implementation planning exercises in Chapter 8 to avoid asking your engineers to tackle poorly articulated problems.

Of all of the machine learning approaches currently in use, supervised machine learning produces the most business value. The core of supervised machine learning is a mathematical **model** that describes how an algorithm makes predictions after being trained with historical data. The goal of **training** is to develop a model capable of mapping each **input** to a target **output**. Let's say you want to predict whether customers visiting your e-commerce site will make a purchase or leave without one. The input should be customer data, which your model will use to make a prediction of whether a particular customer will "buy" or "leave" as the output. In order to properly train this model, you will need to have a large, clearly-labeled dataset of past customer behavior from which the model can learn.

A typical machine learning process follows these steps:

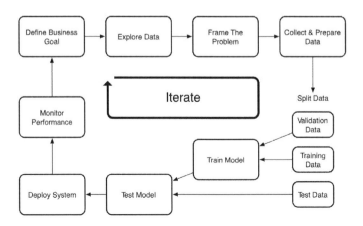

Define Business Goal

Carefully define your highest priority goal and your key performance indicators (KPI). Keep in mind that optimizing for everything means optimizing for nothing. Choosing too many KPIs will invariably result in conflicts where trying to boost one leads to a performance drop in another. Try to balance internal business metrics, such as revenue, with metrics related to the customer experience. Avoid vague requests, such as "increase revenue." Increasing revenue could result from entering new markets, cross-promoting products, or reducing customer churn, all of which will require different technical approaches.

Examine Existing Data and Processes

If your new model depends on existing data and processes, then you will need to perform exploratory analysis to understand the nature of your assets, which will inform your machine learning approach in turn. You may find that your data is insufficient or unsuitable for your objectives, requiring your team to collect new data that specifically addresses your problem.

Frame the Problem

Once you have defined your priority business goal and KPI, and you've identified data and technology dependencies, then your data scientists and engineers can frame your problem in machine learning terms. They can determine how best to prepare your data, which technical approach to take (e.g., supervised vs. unsupervised learning), and develop a hypothesis about the algorithms that will perform best.

Centralize Data

If your desired data resides in different data warehouses or across various departments, it will require a coordinated, cross-functional effort to collate everything into a single training dataset. If you are missing data, you'll need to coordinate with additional teams to define how you want to capture new information across your products, services, and analytics workflows.

Clean Data

Prepare the data for processing by filling in missing values and correcting flaws. Depending on the initial state of the data, you may spend significant amounts of time cleaning and reshaping the raw data into a usable format. For example, locations such as "NYC" may need to be relabeled as "New York City" or with longitude and latitude, and timestamps may need to be converted if they come from different time zones. Many data scientists lament that they spend the majority of their time on data cleaning, but it must be done.

Split Data

If you use all of your data to train a model, then you cannot easily check to see if that model will perform well on new data. To estimate your generalization error, or the error rate that your model will have while analyzing new data, you will need to randomly split the available data into three sets: training data, validation data, and test data. Training data is the baseline data used to build your model. Validation data is used as an intermediate testing set that will be used iteratively improve model performance. Once you have tuned your model to an acceptable performance level, use test data to estimate your model's generalization ability.

Train Model

Model training begins once the data has been split and algorithmic approaches are selected. Experienced data scientists and machine learning engineers may have some sense as to which models work best for specific problems and data types, but machine learning remains as much an art as a science. Finding the best fit will probably be require testing a variety of algorithms, and your team may be surprised by what works best.

Validate and Test Model

Measure the model's accuracy by using your validation and test datasets. Metrics for accuracy include recall and precision, discussed earlier in this chapter. You will repeat training and testing until you find the best model that produces the desired performance results.

Deploy Model

Finally, deploy the model in your business to reap the benefits of this new technology. Successful models are used to recommend products, customize landing pages, or score new sales leads.

Monitor Performance

Machine learning models will decay in performance if they are not regularly retrained on fresh data. You must monitor both a model's performance as well as the integrity of its data inputs. If undetected, corrupt data may not manifest in your predictions until later, which is why it is important to carefully track your data. Changes in data pipelines, data structure, or external conditions all need to be addressed, or they may affect the accuracy of your model.

Iterate

Machine learning models are never "done," in the sense that they will need continuous monitoring, iteration, and retraining to maintain required levels of performance over time. You may find that your original business goals and performance targets will shift in response to exogenous events or based on what you learn from previous models.

Maintain an Experimental Mindset

Science experiments fail 99 percent of the time. As an executive, you'd be fired if you failed 99 percent of the time. Corporate risk aversion prevents most business leaders from leading bold experiments. However, early AI investments can be classified as R&D spending, and they should be regarded as innovation opportunities with potentially exponential returns.

Consistent testing and iteration are critical to AI systems that learn and improve over time. The vast majority of tests will fail initially. When IBM Watson collaborated with Toyota to create advertising copy for the new Mirai car model, the first versions of algorithmically generated texts were incoherent. After a couple months of tuning, the AI system learned to write thousands of useful ads.[81]

11. EXPERIMENT AND ITERATE

Building artificial intelligence does not have to involve big data, a large team, or expansive changes. Since machine learning processes are iterative and improve over time, you can start small and slowly expand your resources.

Agile Development

Agile software development is a time-boxed, iterative approach to building software incrementally. In a traditional waterfall software development model, a product is delivered in its entirety at the end of a project. By contrast, agile processes break down a project into tiny chunks of user functionality that can be addressed in two- to four-week-long cycles called sprints. This strategy uses continuous review to identify potential for improvement after every sprint.

The flexibility of an agile development process works well for developing products that use AI. Anand Rao, Innovation Lead for US Analytics at PwC, and his team use the agile method to run four-week sprints on AI projects, during which they transform an idea into an initial implementation.[82] After each cycle, the team reviews project performance to determine whether the project needs more data or is even worth pursuing further. As Rao explains, this iterative process "gives the option to the client to experiment in a bite-size piece, as opposed to big chunk investments," thereby mitigating risk. PwC uses efficient teams of only two or three people and runs up to 80 sprints a year.

Technical Debt

Building a successful machine learning model is just the first step to creating an AI product. In a conference paper titled "The Hidden Technical Debt In Machine Learning Systems," Google engineers warn that writing the code for a model constitutes only a small fraction of the engineering required for producing a machine learning system.[83] The vast majority of the engineering required to productize a model lies in developing and maintaining the vast and complex infrastructure that surrounds the code.

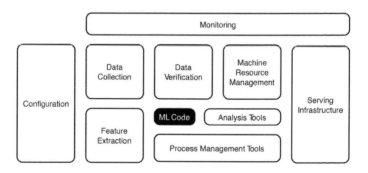

Just as a minor credit card balance can snowball into an unpayable debt over time, poor software design decisions made at the beginning of a project can easily compound into costly problems in the future. Technical debt refers to the cost of additional rework that will be needed in the future when you opt for quick and hacky fixes early on. In machine learning, you can easily incur massive ongoing systems costs by failing to mitigate risks early in the development process.[84]

Your most talented data scientists and machine learning engineers want to build new models. Few of them are dedicated to the unsexy tasks of maintaining existing models. However, the performance of your existing models will deteriorate as environmental conditions change over time. For example, as your e-commerce inventory changes, your recommender system will need to learn to suggest new products to shoppers.

As more machine learning algorithms are put into production, you will also need to dedicate more resources to model maintenance—monitoring, validating, and updating the model. A myriad of dependencies lead to machine learning debt, with certain practices incurring more technical debt than others. According to Google researchers, contributing factors include "probabilistic variables, data dependencies, recursive feedback loops, pipeline processes, configuration settings, and other factors that exacerbate the unpredictability of machine learning algorithm performance."[85]

Machine learning debt can be divided into three main types: code debt, data debt, and math debt.[86] Code debt arises from the need to revisit and repurpose older code that may no longer suit the project. Data debt focuses on the data that was used to train the algorithm, which may have been incorrect or is no longer relevant. For example, a model predicting consumer healthcare coverage may flounder when healthcare regulations change, as new regulatory mandates decrease the importance of historical data, or when historical data must be purged for reasons of compliance. Finally, math debt stems from the complexity of the model's algorithms. Most machine learning algorithms will require ongoing customizations that can make them harder to configure, maintain, and understand.

Deployment and Scaling

In order to support a large number of enterprise-wide machine learning systems, you will need a centralized technology architecture that provides a stable development and deployment environment. Companies such as Google, Facebook, and AirBnB have created internal Machine Learning as a Service (MLaaS) platforms to enable their engineering teams to build, deploy, and operate machine learning solutions with ease. These MLaaS systems, also known as end-to-end machine learning platforms, reduce the time required to push models to production from months to weeks.

The size and scale of Uber's operations—over 5.5 million rides per day[87]—created a number of challenges for their machine learning models. In the beginning, development was decentralized, with data scientists using a variety of tools to create predictive models while engineers built one-off systems to bring these models into production. There were no standardized knowledge databases, no centralized data pipelines, and no streamlined production process. Uber developed the Michelangelo MLaaS platform to address these issues. Similar internal platforms at other companies include Google's TFX and Facebook's FBLearner Flow.

MLaaS systems are designed to encompass the entire machine learning workflow: data management, algorithm training, evaluation and deployment, and model iteration. They standardize the workflows and tools across engineering, data science, and research functions, enabling teams to easily build and operate machine learning systems at scale. Successful MLaaS systems also grow with the business and adapt to new data sources, processes, algorithms, and tools.

MLaaS also facilitates clear knowledge documentation. The following types of data are captured by Uber's Michelangelo[88]:

- Who trained the model
- Start and end time of the training job (some

complicated training jobs can take hours
or even days)

- Full model configuration (features used, hyper-
parameter values, etc.)
- Reference to training and test datasets
- Model accuracy metrics
- Standard charts and graphs for each model type
- Full learned parameters for the model
- Summary statistics for model visualization
- Other notes and information

Overall, successful MLaaS systems have the following characteristics[89]:

- **Algorithm-agnostic**. The platform supports
numerous machine learning algorithms and
innovative combinations of these algorithms.
- **Reusable**. Each machine learning algorithm can
be reused in other applications.
- **Simple.** The system is easy for engineers
of varying levels of technical experience to
understand and use. Over time, the steps should
become fully automated.
- **Centralized knowledge**. Information on past
experiments, including results, is easily accessible
for future reference.
- **Flexible**. The platform is capable of handling a

variety of data types and learning tasks specific to
your company and industry.

- **Reliable and scalable.** The platform remains
  resilient and be able to scale with high
  volumes of data during both the training and
  production phases.

- **Intuitive user interface** (**UI**). The system has
  a simple user interface to allow engineers and
  even non-technical domain experts to easily
  manage experiments as well as visualize and
  compare outputs.

Iteration and Improvement

Machine learning models are not static. Your model will
need to be retrained as new data becomes available or
as external conditions change. The frequency of updates
will depend on your algorithm, the situation, and the
availability of data. If you are building a spam email filter,
then you may need to retrain constantly if spammers are
constantly formulating new attacks. If you are modeling
user churn in e-commerce, then you may not need to
update the model as frequently if customers are slow to
change in their turnover behavior.

Models are typically retrained every few weeks or months,
or when there is a substantial change in external conditions
that fundamentally changes the model trajectory. Some

use cases may require daily or even real-time retraining. As a rule of thumb, half of your time should be spent on measurements and maintenance rather than on model creation. While these tasks are not as exciting as building new models, they are just as important when it comes to servicing your machine learning debt.

As these complexities pile up over time, you will likely find it more challenging to conduct root-cause analyses that are vital for maintenance. The black box nature of many deep learning algorithms makes it even more difficult to determine how an algorithm made a particular decision. Therefore, continuous monitoring and servicing of your models will be vital to maintaining the health of your machine learning systems.

Tools and techniques for building and deploying enterprise-scale machine learning models are constantly evolving. Visit our website at **appliedaibook.com** for updated resources on successfully managing machine learning projects.

AI for Enterprise Functions

12. OBSTACLES AND OPPORTUNITIES

"AI is like teenage sex. Everyone talks about it. Nobody knows how to do it. But everyone thinks everyone else is doing it, so they claim to do it too." —Internet meme

Everybody claims to have "AI" in their products today. There are "AI-powered" juicers, "AI-enabled" wifi routers, "AI-enhanced" baby cameras. We were even pitched an "AI standing desk" that memorizes your work habits and automatically orders your lunch.

To be fair, no global company today survives without using the Internet, email, or mobile devices. These previous technology innovations have become ubiquitous, even mundane, and AI will likely follow suit. Data, digital transformation, and machine intelligence will simply be table stakes for any organization that wants to stay competitive in an increasingly automated world.

Sadly, market hype about AI has made it trendy to brag about using AI without any understanding or experience. We once spoke to an executive who boasted about being the "leader in AI" in his industry. His justification? He managed to buy software from an external vendor who provides commodity speech-to-text transcription. And the purchasing process only took several months!

Don't be this person. Despite marketing or PR claims, buying a tool from a third-party vendor will not magically make your organization a "leading AI company." Right now, only a handful of leading technology companies— i.e. Google, Facebook, Microsoft, and Amazon—possess the culture, talent, and infrastructure to innovate at the cutting edge of artificial intelligence. Not only have they hired the world's most brilliant AI talent to staff research groups like Google Brain, DeepMind, and Facebook AI Research (FAIR), they've also developed powerful internal machine learning platforms like Facebook's FBLearner, Uber's Michelangelo, Google's TFX, and Twitter's Cortex to enable their engineers and other employees to rapidly develop models and capabilities into product teams, business units, and end-user experiences.

While your organization is probably not going to turn into Google overnight, decisions and investments that you make today will dramatically affect your ability to adopt machine intelligence in the future. Weaving modern AI advances into your organization requires executive commitment, deep technical understanding, new organizational capabilities, openness to experimentation, and lots and lots (and lots) of data.

Enterprise functions represent one of the easiest entry

points for deploying AI within your own company. Though not as attention-grabbing as the latest breakthrough research in neural network architectures, finding ways to deploy existing AI techniques to optimize common business functions is usually easier than brainstorming new projects. Multiple products targeted at inefficiencies in virtually every enterprise function are already on the market, promising to revolutionize how we work.

To help you navigate through the complex range of AI solutions, we created an Enterprise AI Landscape to track leading companies that have deployed machine learning solutions to streamline their business functions. You can access the guide on our website at **appliedaibook. com/resources**.

Current Obstacles

Companies generate revenue by either cutting costs or finding new ways to make money, with the first being generally more straightforward than the second. Current AI-based solutions are very good at reducing inefficiencies in the workplace. By handing off repetitive tasks to software, employees have more time and energy to spend on high-value tasks.

Unfortunately, for companies that do not have technology as a core competency, even getting started can be a daunting task. In Chapter 6, "Building an AI-Ready

Culture," we talked about the obstacle that is the HiPPO—the highest paid person's opinion—which allows gut instinct to override available data when determining company direction and policy. Unfamiliarity with AI may lead the HiPPO to reject any suggestions for adoption. While this strategy may produce a feeling of security in the short term, it also increases the probability of failure in the long term.

Even after getting past the HiPPO resistance, investigating what's being offered on the market today can be a daunting task. AI-based solutions are complex technical products, and you may be asked to choose between vague product descriptions that are heavy on buzzwords but light on exposition or the reverse—convoluted technical descriptions that don't actually tell you what the products do. The resulting confusion increases the risk of buying a product that doesn't actually address your company's needs.

Does your company have enough data to train a new model? Modern AI solutions are voracious, requiring clean and relevant data by the bucketful. As a rule of thumb, if you can load all of the data that you've collected so far into Excel and clean it by hand, then you probably don't have enough data for robust machine learning applications.

AI solutions are also not cheap. The huge initial outlay of cash can take years to achieve its anticipated ROI, if at all, especially if your company experiences decreased productivity during implementation. The combination of all of these factors can be daunting to interested companies that have no incentive to look beyond their next quarterly earnings report.

Ultimately, integrating an AI-based solution into the workflow of an enterprise function, one of the vital cogs that keep your business running, is a major undertaking. While established technology companies recognize that technical investments take a long time to mature and can afford to wait for success, your company may be less happy about weathering the disruptions. Don't do it unless you already have a defined plan of implementation, allies in the C-Suite to champion that plan, and mutually agreed-upon evaluation metrics at incremental deadlines.

What AI Can Do for Enterprise Functions

Current AI-based solutions are very good at streamlining processes and taking over rote tasks such as triggering a workflow. Automation frees up the cognitive load of your employees so that they can focus on more meaningful aspects of their jobs. For example, mundane tasks can take up to 75 percent of a recruiter's job. Handing off the responsibility of filtering resumés, which consists primarily of matching terms or looking for specific experiential phrases, to an AI-based solution can free up to half of the recruiter's day for other tasks. Recruiters can then use the extra time to get better acquainted with existing candidates, thereby improving the overall hiring process.

Similar redundancies exist across all enterprise functions, and this section will discuss some of the most common opportunities for optimization that currently exist. We hope that these examples will inspire you as you assess your own organization for potential implementation opportunities.

13. GENERAL AND ADMINISTRATIVE

General and administrative units such as Finance, Legal, and Business Operations are often underappreciated because they do not generate revenue. However, these functions perform some of the most critical jobs within the company, such as keeping track of the money that Sales bring in, using that money to pay for the ads that Marketing will use to attract new leads, and keeping a wary eye out for regulatory and legal hurdles that Product Management may have to address.

General and administrative roles are riddled with tedious but critical tasks such as manual data entry, which requires extreme precision. The exponentially-increasing volume of data combined with limits on the human capacity for sustained attention to detail is a recipe for corporate disaster. Fortunately, computers do not tire and excel at repetitive tasks where attention to detail is essential.

Finance and Accounting

Instead of forcing your human employees to spend

hours over a spreadsheet to audit financial line items for duplicates, errors, expense abuses, and spending anomalies, you can use natural language processing software such as AppZen to automate expense management for accountants and controllers. This cuts down on the possibility of error and removes the most tedious parts of an accounting professional's job. For employees who must regularly submit expense reports, Expensify saves time and cuts down on error by streamlining business travel booking and expense reporting procedures.

How much is your company spending on lightbulbs, and is your supplier charging too much for them? Spend analysis collects, cleans, and analyzes expenditure data to improve operating efficiency and to decrease waste. Large companies tend to be populated with multiple record-keeping systems, all of them incompatible with each other, and the threat of missing data looms large. Specialist platforms like Coupa leverage machine learning to better recognize and categorize spending data, even filling in missing information to create a clean, standardized overview of a company's spending patterns.

Legal and Compliance

Legal technology, also known as LegalTech, is already a $16 billion market in the US, and the biggest change in this market has been the rapid rise of AI-powered products. As with other General and Administrative functions, AI's greatest utility lies in the automation of tedious manual processes, allowing lawyers, particularly those working in-house, to devote more time to valuable and strategic work.

The biggest challenge, however, is one of tradition. The legal sector devoting a great deal of attention as well as skepticism to LegalTech. Legal lags behind other service-based industries when it comes to automating tasks. LegalTech market is a small piece of the total US legal services market, which is worth $437 billion.[90] Research shows that 75 percent of law firms spend somewhere between zero and four percent of their total revenue on technology, as compared to 5.2 percent for the average company.

Current applications include drafting and reviewing contracts, mining documents in discovery and due diligence, sifting data to predict outcomes, and answering routine questions. In-house legal departments can spend 50 percent of their time reviewing contracts,[91] creating bottlenecks that slow down business transactions. AI solutions using natural language processing (NLP) can act as spotter to provide needed information on contract terms, allowing lawyers to focus their attention on the most critical segments of each contract and shortening the overall legal clearance process.

Legal teams must ensure that contracts are not hiding obligations, liabilities, or legal exposures. In addition, legal teams must also stay up-to-date with ever-changing compliance rules. AI-powered due diligence agents are already being used to review billions of dollars in mergers and acquisitions (M&A) transactions as well as to extract and manage data of multinational corporations in multiple languages.[92]

Legal research can now be supplemented by AI-powered assistants that can review and categorize large bodies of documents, flagging the most important ones for human attention. New products, including ones making use of IBM Watson, can now respond to legal questions in plain English, even outperforming experienced legal professionals in accuracy, efficiency, and user satisfaction.[93] Tools can now predict how courts may rule on new cases, such as those dealing with tax law, with an accuracy rate of more than 90 percent.[94]

Your company's intellectual property is often your most valuable asset. AI can now assist with invention disclosures, docketing, deadlines, filing applications, valuing your IP portfolio, and budgeting. According to lawyers for IBM, the use of AI has cut down on the total time needed to analyze trademark search results by 50 percent.[95] Other uses include spotting warning signs of burgeoning legal issues, which may ultimately help to preserve and increase the value of your brand portfolio.

Last, expertise automation, the intelligent automation of legal expertise and processes, provides a simple way of creating walkthroughs or virtual assistants for compliance and regulatory matters in a particular sector or legal field. Unlike human lawyers, expertise automation software do not have set business hours, making it easier to access legal knowledge to answer common questions.

Records Maintenance

The primary use case in administrative roles is form processing and records maintenance, which involves countless hours of accurate data entry. We've probably all run into organizations that continue to insist on handwritten forms that some poor intern must then painstakingly enter into legacy databases. The need for manual entry creates a bottleneck and increases the risk of error, especially as the prevalence of keyboards has sent handwriting legibility into a steep decline. To deal with this problem, HyperScience utilizes advanced computer vision techniques to scan and process handwritten forms to eliminate the data entry bottleneck. Once a form is scanned, their software cleans the image, matches the format to the correct form, then extracts and stores the relevant information in the correct database.

General Operations

Most companies have tons of repetitive digital workflows. These workflows can be tedious to complete. Employees responsible for these tasks can easily become bored and inattentive, allowing errors to creep into your operations and your data.

Fortunately, these tasks are well-suited for automation by Robotic Process Automation (RPA), which are software robots programmed to perform a specified sequence of actions. Even better, RPA deployment is relatively fast and low risk, so that problematic robots can quickly be removed without detriment to existing systems. Examples of workflows at which RPAs excel include performing regular diagnostics of your software or hardware, creating and updating accounting records (such as payroll), or automatically generating and delivering periodic reports to the relevant stakeholders.

The first RPAs were simple programmable bots that required very specific inputs. They were inflexible, and changes in any step required that the robot be reprogrammed. More recent versions that have self-learning and NLP capabilities can now learn from example, to the point where RPAs can recognize the existence of new input and ask for help. Unfortunately, AI-based RPAs need to learn from experience, meaning that this ability to recognize new inputs is still dependent on having access to large amounts of previously generated data.

14. HUMAN RESOURCES AND TALENT

The foundation of every company is its people, and we believe that hiring good people who work well together is the most important component to a successful company. Finding and retaining the right people is not easy, and talent development is an ongoing strategic priority for most companies. Though Human Resources and Talent are generally considered General and Administrative roles, we discuss them separately due to the sheer number of use cases available for optimization.

Matching Candidates to Positions

Specialists traditionally spend much of their time and energy manually identifying candidates, drawing up compensation packages, designing career plans for new hires, and creating the right corporate culture so that employees can feel comfortable and work productively. Though this model generates a lot of records on prospective hires as well as on both current and former employees, decisions are made primarily by combining intuition with market data.

Fortunately, the nature of HR, which emphasizes matching and planning skills, and the abundance of internal data create opportunities for AI-based optimization throughout the hiring process. Recruiting and hiring platforms like Scout, Entelo, UpScored, and SAP's SuccessFactors help match, discover, and find candidates based on desired skills and additional criteria. These platforms use a variety of AI techniques, such as algorithmic matching and predictive scanning, to identify promising candidates.

Because these tools are optimized for skills, values, and experience, their use can help reduce unconscious biases that deter us from making the best hiring decisions, in the process promoting diversity and a more inclusive corporate culture. Both Talent Sonar and Textio seek to improve the hiring process by first leveraging predictive analytics to create more informative and attractive job ads, thereby attracting more applicants, and then by providing a platform for identity-blind resumé review and evaluation, producing a qualified and diverse candidate pool.

Managing the Interview Process

While the interview process is a slightly different experience with every new candidate, automation can streamline many steps within the process. Companies like Wade & Wendy and HireVue use AI to automate candidate communication and assessments, allowing hiring managers to gather more information about each candidate while also scaling up hiring efforts.

Intelligent Scheduling

Scheduling a meeting often requires a lengthy email exchange and the help of one or several human assistants. Products that incorporate natural language processing (NLP) can be used to analyze the contents of email exchanges, extract schedule preferences, and automatically set meetings. Both of the platforms mentioned in the section above take advantage of intelligent scheduling, eliminating the need for lengthy email exchanges to synchronize schedules.

Career Planning and Retention Risk Analysis

Like customer retention, hiring can be a complicated process. HR must match an open position with the right person who has the required skills. Once hired, HR and the employee then face the new challenge of mapping out a career plan and trajectory that is desirable to both parties. This process may become more challenging if an employee expresses a desire to develop in areas where the company has no open positions. An employee may become dissatisfied and look for jobs elsewhere if that person's skill set was badly matched with the demands of the job or finds no opportunities forthcoming. Companies like the HR ERP giant Workday and emerging player HiQ apply data science and machine learning methods to understand risk factors and improve retention.

Administrative Functions

HR specialists must balance strategic assignments with tedious administrative tasks. While they may be given important assignments, such as designing company-wide initiatives about culture or mapping out career trajectories for existing employees, they are also interrupted constantly to service more mundane requests, such as answering questions about workplace policy, filing paperwork, or entering information into databases. The competing demands can result in a highly inefficient and frustrating work environment.

As with the hiring process, the repetitive nature of these administrative tasks is well suited to automation. Companies like Talla use AI to take over the servicing of administrative questions and requests. Employees get answers to routine questions more quickly, while HR specialists get more time and mental firepower to devote to creating high-value deliverables.

15. BUSINESS INTELLIGENCE AND ANALYTICS

Business intelligence (BI) creates meaning from data that your company collected. The goal is to leverage that meaning to guide future business decisions. For example, your company may want to know whether a specific product is selling well, and knowing that the 18- to 25-year-old demographic loves your product will affect how that product will be marketed in the future. Similarly, if BI finds that your employees are bored because their skills are being underutilized, HR can use that knowledge to adjust individual advancement plans, increasing employee satisfaction in the process.

Data Wrangling

To create meaning, BI must first convert data into information, then analyze that information to create insights that can then be converted into recommendations for action. Pieces of data can be as simple as the purchasing history of one customer, and they hold very little meaning on their own. Data becomes valuable when all of the pieces have been gathered together, because then technical specialists can structure that collection in ways that aid pattern-matching. Now, a single customer's purchases can be understood in the context of all the purchases that all customers have ever made. Analysts can then draw more general conclusions about product performance and suggest ways to improve sales.

Traditionally, technical specialists had to manually record, prepare, analyze, and interpret the data. This is a labor-intensive process because a company generates a large volume of data, and human involvement incurs the constant risk of error. Data preparation, which cleans, labels, and structures your data for consistency and accuracy, is the most important step in BI. Without clean data, your analysis will not be accurate, and you should not have confidence in your conclusions. However, data preparation is work-intensive and tedious, and few data scientists enjoy the drudgery.

Advances in AI mean that many of these tasks can now be done automatically and much more accurately than before. Multiple companies such as Paxata and Trifacta now offer AI-powered data wrangling services that automate portions of the data preparation process, using algorithms and machine learning to transform raw data inputs into well-labeled data structures that are ready for use. These companies emphasize ease of use. Paxata, for example, offers an Excel-like UI, while Trifacta offers a proprietary interface that encourages users to visually interact with their data.

Data Architecture

While centralized data allows the company to more efficiently and more intelligently assess its overall state of being, the process of collecting that data is complicated by the existence of data silos. Different business units generate data at different rates and in different, often incompatible, formats. What's more, the existence of whatever was generated is often not common knowledge to the rest of the company.

The existence of data silos are a manifestation of turf wars between business units. Business units have wildly different sets of priorities and goals. In more dysfunctional companies, they may perceive themselves to be in active competition for resources with other units and refuse to sharing data in order to protect their proprietary information.

Whatever the reason, data silos are a bad idea. While a data silo may provide a deep, micro-level dive into the performance of one particular group, these insights do not exist in the context of the information being generated by the rest of the company, making it hard to make holistic, data-driven decisions. For example, data-sharing between Sales and Marketing can give Marketing a better understanding of the types of leads that are actually converting to sales, while Sales gets better information about customer segments that salespeople should prioritize.

Who owns the data if everyone contributes to it? In more pessimistic terms, who's responsible if something goes wrong? Accountability is clear when a business unit can appoint one owner for its siloed data, but it is less clear when a dataset consists of multiple contributions from multiple departments or is of equal interest to multiple units. For example, Product Management, Sales, and Marketing all want chatbot data on customer interactions, but there is no clear owner when the results are important to all three units.

As a result of the need to manage data that is increasing in scope and complexity and being generated by multiple business units across an organization, new jobs specializing in the care and feeding of shared data have appeared. Chief Data Officer (CDOs) and Chief Data Scientist positions are now becoming common in companies, especially those interested in championing new AI investments. For companies that do not have the capacity or the desire to tackle data silos on their own, companies like Maana, Alation, and Tamr offer ML-powered data unification and cataloguing services.

Analytics

Now that all of the available data has been unearthed and cleaned, you are now ready to leverage the fruits of your labor into sweet, sweet knowledge. Are your employees happy? Are your operational processes as efficient as they can be? Is your current business strategy still the right business strategy? Having the right data can help you to answer all of these questions *and more.*

Unfortunately, the relatively small talent pool that we discussed in Chapter 7 means that you may have a hard time filling positions even if you're not doing state-of-the-art AI research. If you want to make a trial run to see what AI can do for your data, or you don't know whether you want to initiate a search for in-house talent, many companies now offer AI-powered analytical services. Ayasdi and Kyndi leverage different machine learning algorithms to extract patterns and make predictions on your company's data, while DataSift specializes in sifting through and classifying natural language textual data to track social sentiments.

16. SOFTWARE DEVELOPMENT

Software development is no exception to the AI revolution. Not only can machine learning techniques be used to accelerate the traditional software development lifecycle (SDLC), they also present a completely new paradigm for inventing technology.

In traditional development, you have to specify the exact functionality of your computer program before coding it by hand. However, many tasks, such as categorizing objects in a photo, are far too complex to teach to computers in a rigid, rule-based manner.

AI techniques such as machine learning and deep learning instead rely on learning algorithms that are iteratively trained and continuously improved on curated, domain-specific data. This training allows them to deduce which features and patterns are important without being explicitly taught this knowledge. This quality makes them better than the best human-engineered code in analyzing image/video, sound/speech, and text.

The most profound impact of AI on computer

programming has been the unraveling of how humans perceive, define, and execute software development. Pete Warden, a research engineer at Google, predicts that "in ten years I predict most software jobs won't involve programming." [96] Andrej Karpathy, the Director of AI at Tesla, offers a similar vision, describing a future in which "a large portion of programmers of tomorrow do not maintain complex software repositories, write intricate programs, or analyze their running times. They collect, clean manipulate, label, analyze and visualize data that feeds neural networks." [97]

The traditional development lifecycle for "Software 1.0" typically starts with a tech spec, which defines functionality requirements for a product. The tech spec is then passed to design and development to guide the development of viable prototypes. QA testing scrutinizes the final candidate for muster before deploying it to production, where the product must be continuously maintained. Over time, a program can grow in complexity, requiring multiple dependencies and integrations as well as layers upon layers of functionalities and interfaces. All of these components must be manually managed and updated, which can lead to inconsistencies and unresolvable bugs.

Machine learning-driven development, or "Software 2.0," extrapolates important features and patterns in data and builds mathematical models that leverage these insights. According to Karpathy, Software 2.0 is code written by machine learning methods such as stochastic gradient descent and backpropagation instead of being generated by humans. In traditional software development, adding functionality always requires manual engineering work. In machine learning, adding functionality can be as simple as re-training your model on new data.

While machine learning development has its own debugging and maintenance challenges, it also offers many benefits, including increased homogeneity, ease of management, and high portability. On the flip side, the complexity of these models will make it difficult for humans to fully comprehend how they work, leading them to appear as "black boxes." Worse, the complexity may hide algorithmic biases that can lead to unintended and embarrassing consequences.

Software 2.0 will not supplant traditional software development entirely. Training a machine learning model is only a single step in the development process. As discussed in our section on technical debt in Chapter 11, the machine learning code is only a small fraction of any AI system. Critical components such as data management, front-end product interfaces, and security will still need to be handled by regular software.

We've listed a few areas in which technologies developed using the traditional SDLC can benefit from machine learning approaches. According to a Forrester Research report on the impact of AI in software development, the bulk of the interest in applying AI to software development lies in automated testing and bug detection tools.[98]

Rapid Prototyping

Turning business requirements into actual products typically require months, if not years, of planning. Machine learning has shortened this process by enabling non-specialists to develop technologies using either natural language or visual interfaces.

Intelligent Programming Assistants

Developers spend the vast majority of their time reading documentation or debugging code. Smart programming assistants can reduce the time spent on these tasks by offering just-in-time support and recommendations, such as relevant specifications, best practices, and code examples. Examples of such assistants include Kite for Python and Codota for Java.

Automatic Analytics and Error Handling

Programming assistants can also learn from past experiences to identify common errors and flag them automatically during development. Once a technology has been deployed, machine learning can be used to analyze system logs to flag errors. In the future, it may be possible to allow software to modify itself without human intervention in response to errors.

Automatic Code Refactoring

Clean code is critical for team collaboration and long-term

maintenance. Large-scale code refactoring is often an unavoidable necessity as enterprises upgrade to new technologies. Machine learning can be used to analyze code and automatically optimize it for interpretability and performance.

Precise Estimates

Software development has a reputation for exceeding budget and planned timelines. Reliable estimates require deep expertise, understanding of context, and familiarity with the implementation team. Machine learning can be trained on data from past projects—such as user stories, feature definitions, estimates, and actuals—to more accurately predict the effort and budget that will be required.

Strategic Decision-Making

Which products and features should you prioritize, and which ones should you cut? An AI solution trained on past developments and current business priorities can assess the performance of existing applications, helping you and your engineering teams to identify efforts that will maximize impact and minimize risk.

17. MARKETING

Unlike the previous units that primarily generate value through cost-cutting, both Marketing and Sales are directly responsible for generating revenue. This unique position gives the two functions significantly more power to direct investment into new projects. The need to keep up with competitors in fighting for market share means that both units are, on average, much more willing to try new tools as well.

Marketing and Sales work hand-in-hand to attract and retain customers, which requires understanding what interests customers and motivates them to want to buy products. The goal overlap between them means that they share many tools, though they are applied to different use cases. For example, Marketing may want to use natural language generation products to generate ad copy that increases click rates, while Sales may want to use the same product to create sales pitch email headers that prospective customers will actually want to read.

Marketing aims to educate consumers by communicating about your company's products and services, your brand,

and the values that you stand for. Catching and retaining the attention of today's fickle customers will require your company to have accurate consumer research to build your branding strategy, create engaging content to excite interest in your audience, and understand how consumers will weigh your message against those of your fiercest competitors.

Marketing depends on extensive digital advertising to generate goodwill toward your brand and your products. This is an especially important operation for B2C companies that don't necessarily control the retail channels through which their products are sold. What's more, B2C companies often do not have access to the type of consumer data that retailers have access to. Fortunately, digital products can now capture more data about every user interaction, enabling richer analysis and insights to be derived using machine learning approaches that offer superior accuracy to previous methods. The value of new models can also be tested and measured quickly, leading to a direct impact on revenue and costs. However, the sheer number of individual buyers also means that B2C marketing must weigh individual preferences and the problem of scalability much more heavily.

Digital Ad Optimization

AI research is not yet advanced enough to decipher a person's interests and motivations without human assistance. What is your brand voice and how do you represent that? If customers are angry, how can you make them feel more kindly toward your brand? Because these tasks are less structured, they are much less quantifiable and therefore significantly harder for machines to perform.

However, AI-based content generation, also known as natural language generation (NLG), has been an area of major development in the last few years. We described how IBM Watson was used to create new advertising copy for Toyota in a previous chapter. Machine learning algorithms can now use content from previous marketing campaigns to create emotional profiles for user groups. Based on these profiles, your NLG solution can create similar content that is tailored to specific platforms and to individual user groups, increasing the likelihood that the targeted audience will engage with your ads.

Data about click-through rates can then be fed back to fine-tune your model, building more detailed profiles of how targeted users respond to certain types of messaging. Unlike older A/B testing methods that optimize for statistical significance, AI solutions can be used in real-time, continuous optimization. They work well when you are frequently testing new versions of ads. For example, bandit algorithms, a type of semi-supervised machine learning, are often used to optimize pricing, creative, and placement decisions in digital advertising.

Recommendations and Personalization

Netflix, Amazon, Yelp, and other sophisticated technology companies all use machine learning to improve product recommendations, such as movies to watch, products to buy, or restaurants to try. Personalizing the product selection that you show to customers results in an improved experience for them and higher revenue for you. Many different machine learning approaches are used to drive recommender system performance. Some use active learning in the form of bandit algorithms, like in digital ad optimizations, while others use ensemble methods that combine the advantages of multiple models. Home decor and furniture store West Elm uses an algorithm that reviews a client's Pinterest board to better understand their decor preferences and automatically suggest a shortlist of furniture, rugs, curtains, mirrors, and other items.[99] Stylists at clothing retailer StitchFix uses a computer system to detect the style of a client when suggesting outfits. Extensions of this technology include applications such as Pinterest's Lens and eBay's ShopBot, which recognize items in pictures uploaded by consumers and make recommendations of similar items currently for sale.

The next frontier in recommendation systems is the cold-start scenario, in which algorithms must be able to draw good inferences about users or items despite insufficient information. Layer 6 AI, recently acquired by TD Bank, has focused on making relatively accurate predictions on noisy data in a cold-start scenario.

Customer personalization is like a recommendation system on steroids, delivering highly relevant content, experience, or products to consumers without their having to exert additional effort. Companies such as Monetate, Retail Rocket, BloomReach, and Dynamic Yield now offer personalization engines that use visitor preferences and purchase histories to adjust website content in real-time, highlighting products that are most likely to sell.

18. SALES

Sales, the other side of the traditional revenue-generating coin, aims to convert the interest that Marketing has whipped up into purchases. Your company will need accurate analytics to pinpoint your most likely customers, compelling messages to convert interest into orders, and diligent tending of existing relationships in order to build product and brand loyalty.

Though sales is still largely an intuitive process, based on the ability of a salesperson to accurately infer a customer's needs, your Customer Relations Management software (CRM) holds a treasure trove of data about your company's customer relationships that can be used by machine learning algorithms to improve your sales insights and operations.

Customer Segmentation

Customers have different values, preferences, and behaviors. You may be missing opportunities to make meaningful connections if you treat them the same way.

Even if you haven't defined your segments in advance or are missing labeled data about your target customer behavior, you can use unsupervised machine learning methods to group customers who share common characteristics. Generating clusters of customers in this bottom-up fashion, as compared to defining market segments from the top-down, can detect subtleties of behavior that you may overlook otherwise and help you to identify and qualify new customer segments.

Lead Qualification and Scoring

Lead scoring is typically based on the analysis of static data such as demographics, firmographics, or other behavioral data sources. Because only a few out of thousands of prospective customers ever buy your product, your sales staff need to know how to accurately pinpoint interest and identify the potential for that interest to convert into a sale, or in the best case scenario, repeated sales.

Traditionally, qualifying potential leads requires a salesperson to make cold calls or engage in conversations, first to identify the right decision-maker, and then to assess the possibility of a purchase. However, this process is tedious, and a salesperson has to make a lot of unproductive calls before identifying an actual customer. Recent developments in natural language processing, understanding, and generation enable software to automatically handle outbound queries, process prospect replies, and alert salespeople to high-potential opportunities for follow-up.

Applying sentiment analysis to sales correspondence, for example, can filter through replies to predict the interest level in a potential customer and to pinpoint the best leads. A salesperson can use that analysis to gauge whether a lead is worth the effort for further development, thus avoiding wasted efforts.

Sales Development

Once a lead has been qualified, a salesperson takes over to develop a relationship that will hopefully culminate in a sale. Unfortunately, administrative tedium, such as scheduling demos, follow-ups, and a myriad of other social touch points, can consume a large part of a salesperson's day. Artificial intelligence can be used to analyze the contents of email exchanges, extract schedule preferences, and automatically set meetings. Conversica, for example, uses natural language processing (NLP) to verify contact information, collect purchase requirements, and even set appointments automatically.

Sales Analytics

How much do you think you will sell this year, and how can you improve? You can easily tell if one sales manager is generating far more revenue than her colleagues, but you may not be able to easily discern why. On the surface, the actions of your top performer may look indistinguishable from those of her colleagues. She likely writes emails, makes prospecting calls, and schedules meetings like everyone else. By applying machine learning techniques to all of your sales data, including email content, call transcripts, and CRM engagements, you can train a model to predict which specific actions are likely driving her superior conversions and revenue. These insights can be used to improve your sales playbook for training your entire sales force.

19. CUSTOMER SUPPORT

Customer support has become increasingly important, with analysts predicting that it will overtake product and price as the number one way for a business to differentiate itself by 2020.[100] About 64 percent of consumers now expect real-time responses at any time, and 65 percent say they are likely to switch brands if they receive inconsistent customer service across platforms (online, in-store, phone, text, or via email).[101] However, customer care is expensive. Call centers house hundreds of thousands of agents at a cost of four to twelve dollars per service request.[102] Though customer service has traditionally relied on human empathy to resolve issues, the pressure to keep costs down has made some degree of automation an imperative.

We believe that customer experience is one of the most fruitful areas for the application of artificial intelligence, and machine intelligence can be used to better understand what customers need and to deliver consistently amazing experiences for them.

Conversational Agents

In the face of skyrocketing costs, consumers also expect an ever-higher quality of customer service. While digital assistants have existed for years as curiosities, recent developments in Natural Language Processing (NLP) and integrated technology ecosystems make them increasingly useful. The most popular examples include Amazon Echo's Alexa, Google Assistant, Apple's Siri, and Microsoft's Cortana. Each is tied to a larger network of native software, native hardware, as well as third-party developer additions to add functionality. Conversational agents, also known as bots or chatbots, also exist on popular social media platforms like Facebook Messenger and Tencent's WeChat, enabling us to execute tasks within our messaging environments rather than external websites or apps.

Currently, companies primarily rely on two models to incorporate conversational agents into customer service: the "bot-only" model and the "bot-assisted agent" (or "cyborg") model. In the former model, a conversational computer program interacts directly with a customer without human intervention, while in the latter model, the bot advises the agent on the best course of action or automates agent functions such as knowledge searches.

At present, conversational agents can only handle the most basic service requests, so human agents are still required for complex or difficult cases. Machine learning algorithms can be used to assess customer requests as they arrive, routing easier requests to AI agents while prioritizing higher-value ones for the human staff.

AI solutions also help human agents increase the number of requests that can be addressed. For example, agent autocomplete AIs can offer suggestions to human agents when resolving a ticket, drawing on past conversations to generate automated, intelligent responses to the most common queries.

Meanwhile, startups are competing to provide automated response systems, in which AI agents handles a large portion of requests with minimal human intervention. With improvements in software and AI programming, this field is expected to grow as it represents an ultimate endpoint to the introduction of automation in customer service.

We've compiled a guide that highlights over one hundred different bots from leading brands at **appliedaibook. com/resources**. These bots tackle every aspects of your customer experience and span virtually all industries, ranging from food and entertainment to finance and healthcare.

Social Listening

What are your customers saying about your product and your brand? Sentiment analysis, either using purely statistical methods (less accurate) or machine learning and deep learning methods (significantly more accurate), can gauge the general mood surrounding conversations that your company care about. Natural language processing (NLP) can predict the topic of conversation, the context, as well as the emotional slant and personality characteristics of the content creator.

The proliferation of conversation agents, discussed above, provide a treasure trove of text data such as reviews, comments, social media shares, or customer support tickets for analysis by companies such as Conversocial and Lexalytics. Additional biometrics such as tone, facial expression, and body language can be analyzed if you possess audio or video data.

Customer Churn

Churn occurs when customers fail to complete a critical task for your business model, such as renewing a subscription, pressing the checkout button in their shopping cart, or sharing content with a friend. Supervised learning methods, such as analyzing the difference between free users and paying customers, can help you to identify and analyze the factors that contribute to churn, so that you can proactively re-engage lost customers. For example, irate calls can be routed such that agents are given warning and the customers with the highest flight risk are assisted first.

Lifetime Value

Every business wants to maximize the lifetime value (LTV) of their customers, also known as the net profit that a customer brings you over their entire expected engagement with your company. In order to pass the best leads to your sales teams, you will need to be able to identify the characteristics and behaviors of your most lucrative customers early. With data from your advertising campaigns, acquisition funnel, and customer engagement history, you can use supervised learning methods to predict the best targets.

20. THE ETHICS OF ENTERPRISE AI

This section introduced many ways in which AI can deliver incredible value to enterprise functions. However, while AI will transform the economy on a large scale, not everyone will equally benefit from widespread opportunities that will become available. The new jobs in this economy will require greater technical competency than is currently available in the workforce.

We believe that business leaders have an ethical responsibility to workers to minimize and ameliorate the potential disruptions that AI may bring to the workplace. Intelligent investments in your workforce can increase the likelihood that advanced automation increases productivity while ensuring high levels of employment and shared prosperity.

While Kai-Fu Lee, CEO of Sinovation Ventures, warns that we cannot pretend that AI will not destroy existing jobs,[103] the widespread integration of AI into the workplace will also create the demand for new jobs that require new skills. As AI and robotics increasingly take on the most routine and repetitive tasks in both white-collar and blue-collar industries, jobs that still need human workers will transition from positions that require routine, unskilled labor to ones that require specialized skills and adaptive decision-making abilities. In addition, AI will speed up the pace of automation, in the process requiring workers to learn new skills more quickly in order to stay ahead of the curve.

Workers will need continuous access to high-quality training in order to stay competitive in this new economy. A 2016 White House report on the impact of AI on the economy recommended that high quality, affordable training should start in childhood to prepare students for continued education. Workers going through job transitions will also need ample access to job-driven training and other forms of lifelong learning.[104]

Unfortunately, the United States currently lags behind other industrialized countries on investments in labor market programs, such as training programs or job-search assistance for workers. The White House reported that other OECD countries spent, on average, about 0.6 percent of their GDP on active labor market policies in 2014; in contrast, the United States spent 0.1 percent of its GDP, which was less than half of what was spent thirty years ago.[105] This number is stark especially in light of a recent survey of executives around the world. While 74 percent of respondents said that they would automate their workplaces, only 3 percent said that they would increase investments in worker training![106]

There are signs that this inattention has started to change. Accenture now provides effective retraining programs for its own workforce by leveraging machine learning on resumé content. Algorithms assess whether and when the listed skills may become obsolete, then provide HR with recommendations of skills adjacent to current competencies that workers should acquire.[107] GE's Brilliant Learning Initiative has invested one billion dollars so far into massive open online courses (MOOCs) and immersive programs to help their workers acquire digital skills needed to work with new manufacturing software.[108] German car marker BMW created the BMW Scholars Program, a work-study initiative enables the company's US-based blue collar workers to build new skills while maintaining their jobs.[109]

What kind of jobs will open up in the AI-powered economy? While it is hard to predict the exact nature of the jobs that will be required in the AI-powered enterprise, Paul Daugherty, CTIO at Accenture, believes that we already know the types of skills that will be essential. As AI technology grows increasingly sophisticated, human workers will be needed to train new AI systems, explain the functions of increasingly sophisticated and opaque algorithms so that business leaders can understand how specific recommendations or outcomes are reached, and perform continual maintenance in order to sustain the proper functioning of existing systems. In general, deep technical proficiency, creativity, and learnability will be prized for any job.[110]

Human labor will continue to be needed to supplement functions that have been automated. For example, self-driving vehicles may run into emergencies that must be resolved by human remote operators. In the corporate world, chatbots and customer service AI will need to be built, trained, and pre-programmed with dialog by humans.[111] Moreover, jobs in industries that require complex human interactions and high levels of emotional intelligence, such as those in healthcare and education, will be the least in danger of being automated.[112]

Though the new jobs that will be created by AI will vary widely by industry and function, business leaders must invest in education initiatives immediately in order to minimize future workforce disruptions. Leverage your cross-functional, interdisciplinary AI SWAT team to spot potential blind spots and pitfalls in your organizational design. Connect regularly with front line employees to understand their workflows and their concerns about automation. As we stated in Chapter 14, your people are your most important assets. Invest as much into them as you would invest into your technology to ensure everyone benefits from and succeeds in a world of AI.

We also want to emphasize that enterprise automation affects more than just your employees. In Chapter 4, "The Challenges of Artificial Intelligence," we discussed how AI can harm individuals through unconscious discrimination and malicious disruptions. This potential to cause harm on a massive scale, both accidentally and intentionally, demonstrates the need for executives to be dedicated in ensuring that their AI is designed and deployed in a benevolent fashion.

Developing ethical and safe AI is a complex and ever-evolving topic. While we can write several more additional books to give this subject the attention and coverage that it really needs, business and technology leaders like you can get started by simply making a firm and unwavering commitment to uphold human values and to do no harm with your inventions and practices. Given how quickly technology evolves, you will need to stay vigilant and regularly assess how the AI systems that you are building affect your customers, employees, and society. No profit margin is worth the cost of harming humanity.

SUMMARY AND ADDITIONAL RESOURCES

You've learned about different types of machine intelligence and how to apply them successfully at your organization. You've also been introduced to the incredible array of benevolent applications of AI and to the disastrous consequences of developing technology in an malicious or unethical way. Consciously and carefully designing your AI solutions with a team diverse in viewpoints and experiences will improve your business results and reduce your risk of unintended consequences.

Artificial intelligence is a fast-moving set of technologies. New discoveries, methodologies, and tools are released every day. We have done our best to provide a basic education on planning enterprise AI initiatives successfully, but this is a fast-developing field and we cannot cover all of the details that you need in a single book.

For up-to-date content and case studies on how AI is being used in specific industries, visit our website at **appliedaibook.com**. We track and cover new developments in the field and highlight unique ways in which AI is being applied to solve the world's most pressing problems.

Supplemental content, such as an expanded version of our AI Strategy Framework, can be found at **appliedaibook. com/resources**. If you need executive education for your team and company, you can book a keynote speaker or a workshop at **appliedaibook.com/education**.

To connect with other applied AI professionals, ask questions, and to share knowledge, visit our social communities and discussion forums at **appliedaibook. com/community**.

Your feedback helps us to improve our offerings. If you have spotted errors in this book, would like to suggest improvements to our content, or desire more in-depth coverage of a specific topic, we welcome your thoughts at **authors@appliedaibook.com**.

END NOTES

1. Vincent, J. (2017, October 26). Facebook's head of AI wants us to stop using the Terminator to talk about AI. The Verge. Retrieved from http://www.theverge.com/2017/10/26/16552056/a-intelligence-terminator-facebook-yann-lecun-interview

2. http://fivethirtyeight.com/features/the-real-story-of-2016/

3. Symbolic Artificial Intelligence. (n.d.). In *Wikipedia*. Retrieved November 16, 2017, from http://en.*wikipedia*.org/wiki/Symbolic_artificial_intelligence

4. Le, Q.V., & Schuster, M. (2016, September 27). A Neural Network for Machine Translation, at Production Scale [blog post]. Retrieved from: https://research.googleblog.com/2016/09/a-neural-network-for-machine.html

5. Huang, X.D. (2017, August 20). Microsoft researchers achieve new conversational speech recognition milestone [blog post]. Retrieved from http://www.microsoft.com/en-us/research/blog/microsoft-researchers-achieve-new-conversational-speech-recognition-milestone/

6. Customer Case Studies. (n.d.). Retrieved from http://blog.clarifai.com/customer-case-studies/

7. http://probcomp.csail.mit.edu/

8. Reading List. (n.d.). MIT Probabilistic Computing Project. Retrieved November 16, 2017, from http://probcomp.org/reading-list/

9. Optical computing. (n.d.). In *Wikipedia*. Retrieved November 16, 2017, from http://en.*wikipedia*.org/wiki/Optical_computing

10.   Quantum computing. (n.d.). In *Wikipedia*. Retrieved November 16, 2017, from http://en.*wikipedia*.org/wiki/Quantum_computing

11.   Duhigg, C. (2012, February 16). How Companies Learn Your Secrets. *The New York Times* Magazine. Retrieved from http://www.nytimes.com/2012/02/19/magazine/shopping-habits.html

12.   Simonite, T. (2017, January 18). Google's AI software is learning to make AI software. MIT Technology Review. Retrieved from http://www.technologyreview.com/s/603381/ai-software-learns-to-make-ai-software/

13.   Samim. (2015, November 5). Generating Stories about Images. Retrieved from http://medium.com/@samim/generating-stories-about-images-d163ba41e4ed

14.   Muoio, D. (2016, March 01). These 29 gorgeous images created by Google's AI raised almost $100,000 at auction. *Business Insider.* Retrieved from http://www.businessinsider.com/google-ai-images-raise-100000-at-auction-2016-2

15.   Goleman, D. (2008, March 24). When Emotional Intelligence Does Not Matter More Than IQ. Retrieved from http://www.danielgoleman.info/when-emotional-intelligence-does-not-matter-more-than-iq

16.   Sentiment analysis. (n.d.). In *Wikipedia*. Retrieved on November 17, 2017, from http://en.*wikipedia*.org/wiki/Sentiment_analysis

17.   Knight, W. (2016, June 13). Emotional intelligence might be a virtual assistant's secret weapon. *MIT Technology Review*. Retrieved from http://www.technologyreview.com/s/601654/amazon-working-on-making-alexa-recognize-your-emotions/

18.   Talbot, D. (2014, September 19). Apps for Autism. *MIT Technology Review*. Retrieved from http://www.technologyreview.com/s/528191/digital-summit-first-emotion-reading-apps-for-kids-with-autism/

19.   Technological singularity. (n.d.). In *Wikipedia*. Retrieved November 17, 2017, from http://en.*wikipedia*.org/wiki/Technological_singularity

20. Associated Press. (2012, February 24). Hundreds Of Suicides In India Linked To Microfinance Organizations. *Business Insider.* Retrieved from http://www.businessinsider.com/hundreds-of-suicides-in-india-linked-to-microfinance-organizations-2012-2

21. You, J.X., Li, X.C., Low, M., Lobell, D.B., & Ermon, S. (n.d.). Combining Remote Sensing Data and Machine Learning to Predict Crop Yield. Retrieved from http://sustain.stanford.edu/crop-yield-analysis

22. Zebede, M. & Shahid, S. (2016). Liberia's 'Sex4Grades' Epidemic Is Ruining Children's Lives. *Time.* Retrieved from http://time.com/4282516/liberias-sex4grades-epidemic/

23. Yao, M. (2017, July 11). 5 Ways Humanitarian Bots Can Save The World. *TopBots.* Retrieved from http://www.topbots.com/social-good-humanitarian-bots-can-save-world/

24. Sotomayor, J. (2016, January 8). Success Story: U-Report Liberia exposes Sex 4 Grades in school. Retrieved from http://ureport.in/story/194/

25. Study Finds Computers Surpass Pathologists in Predicting Lung Cancer Type, Severity. (2016). *The ASCO Post.* Retrieved from http://www.ascopost.com/News/43849

26. Patel, T. A., Puppala, M., Ogunti, R. O., Ensor, J. E., He, T., Shewale, J. B., & Chang, J. C. (2016). Correlating mammographic and pathologic findings in clinical decision support using natural language processing and data mining methods. Cancer, 123(1), 114-121. doi:10.1002/cncr.30245

27. As validated against a gold standard review conducted on a sample of records by the study's co-authors, which required 50 to 70 hours.

28. Csail, A. C. (2017, October 16). Using artificial intelligence to improve early breast cancer detection. *MIT News.* Retrieved from http://news.mit.edu/2017/artificial-intelligence-early-breast-cancer-detection-1017

29.   Yao, M. (2017, November 2). Fighting Algorithmic BIAS & Homogenous Thinking in AI. *TopBots*. Retrieved from http://www.topbots.com/fighting-homogenous-thinking-algorithmic-bias-ai/

30.   Westervelt, E (Contributor). (2017, August 18). Did A Bail Reform Algorithm Contribute To This San Francisco Man's Murder? [Radio Broadcast Episode]. In Carline Watson (Executive Producer), *All Things Considered*. Washington, D.C.: NPR. Retrieved from http://www.npr.org/2017/08/18/543976003/did-a-bail-reform-algorithm-contribute-to-this-san-francisco-man-s-murder

31.   Crawford, K. (2016, June 25). Artificial Intelligence's White Guy Problem [Editorial]. *The New York Times*. Retrieved from http://www.nytimes.com/2016/06/26/opinion/sunday/artificial-intelligences-white-guy-problem.html

32.   Sweeney, L. (2013, May). Discrimination in online ad delivery. Communications of the ACM, 56(5), 44-54. doi:10.1145/2447976.2447990

33.   Vafa, K., Haigh, C., Leung, A., & Yonack, N. (2015, September 1). Price Discrimination in The Princeton Review's Online SAT Tutoring Service. *Technology Science*. Retrieved from https://techscience.org/a/2015090102/

34.   Hart, R. (2017, July 10). If you're not a white male, artificial intelligence's use in healthcare could be dangerous. *Quartz*. Retrieved from http://qz.com/1023448/

35.   Brundage, M., et al. (2018, February), The Malicious Use of Artificial Intelligence: Forecasting, Prevention, and Mitigation. Retrieved from https://maliciousaireport.com/

36.   Do we need Asimov's Laws?. (2014, May 16). *MIT Technology Review*. Retrieved from https://www.technologyreview.com/s/527336/do-we-need-asimovs-laws/

37.   Gershgorn, D. (2016, June 3). Google Considers Making A "Big Red Button" To Stop Dangerous A.I. In An Emergency. Popular Science. Retrieved from http://www.popsci.com/google-researches-big-red-button-to-stop-dangerous-ai

38. IEEE Global Initiative on Ethics of Autonomous and Intelligent Systems. (2016, December) Ethically Aligned Design: A Vision for Prioritizing Human Wellbeing with Artificial Intelligence and Autonomous Systems. Retrieved from http://standards.ieee.org/develop/indconn/ec/autonomous_systems.html

39. El Kaliouby, R. Media lunch commentary at the O'Reilly AI Conference on September 18, 2017, in San Francisco, CA.

40. Hebron, P. (2017, April 26). Rethinking Design Tools in the Age of Machine Learning. Retrieved from http://medium.com/artists-and-machine-intelligence/rethinking-design-tools-in-the-age-of-machine-learning-369f3f07ab6c

41. Andreessen, M. (2011, August 20). Why Software Is Eating the World. *Wall Street Journal.* Retrieved from https://www.wsj.com/articles/SB10001424053111903480904576512250915629460

42. Lardinois, F. (2016, September 26). Microsoft CEO Satya Nadella on how AI will transform his company. *Tech Crunch.* Retrieved from http://techcrunch.com/2016/09/26/microsoft-ceo-satya-nadella-on-how-ai-will-transform-his-company/

43. D'Onfro, J. (2016, April 28). Google's vision of the future is a smart assistant that follows you everywhere. *Business Insider* Australia. Retrieved from http://www.businessinsider.com.au/google-sundar-pichai-outlines-focus-in-founders-letter-2016-4

44. Galeon, D. (2017, May 09). Amazon's CEO Says We're Living in the Golden Age of AI. Futurism. Retrieved from http://futurism.com/amazons-ceo-says-were-living-in-the-golden-age-of-ai/

45. Zilis, S. & Cham, J. (2016, November 7) The Current State of Machine Intelligence 3.0. *O'Reilly.* Retrieved from https://www.oreilly.com/ideas/the-current-state-of-machine-intelligence-3-0

46. Leaper, B. (2014, July). The Rise of the Chief Data Officer. *Wired.* Retrieved from https://www.wired.com/insights/2014/07/rise-chief-data-officer/

47.   Purdy, M., & Daugherty, P. (2016) Artificial intelligence is the future
       of growth. (2016). Retrieved from https://www.accenture.com/ca-
       en/insight-artificial-intelligence-future-growth

48.   Ng, A. (2017, April 21). Hiring Your First Chief AI Officer. *Harvard
       Business Review.* Retrieved from http://hbr.org/2016/11/hiring-
       your-first-chief-ai-officer

49.   Interview with Marina Kalika, Director of Solutions Marketing at
       Nuance. Conducted by Adelyn Zhou on April 25, 2017.

50.   Manyika, J., Chui, M., Miremadi, M., Bughin, J., George, K.,
       Willmott, P., & Dewhurst, M. (2017). Harnessing automation for
       a future that works. Retrieved from http://www.mckinsey.com/
       global-themes/digital-disruption/harnessing-automation-for-a-fu-
       ture-that-works

51.   Lohr, S. (2017, January 12). Robots Will Take Jobs, but Not as Fast
       as Some Fear, New Report Says. *The New York Times.* Retrieved from
       http://www.nytimes.com/2017/01/12/technology/robots-will-
       take-jobs-but-not-as-fast-as-some-fear-new-report-says.html

52.   Zhou, A. (2017, October 5). Accenture Augments Human Capital
       With Artificial Intelligence To Stay Competitive. *Forbes.* Retrieved
       from   http://www.forbes.com/sites/adelynzhou/2017/10/04/
       accenture-augments-human-capital-with-artificial-intelli-
       gence-to-stay-competitive/

53.   Metz, C. (2017, October 22). Tech Giants Are Paying Huge Sal-
       aries for Scarce A.I. Talent. *The New York Times.* Retrieved from
       http://www.nytimes.com/2017/10/22/technology/artificial-intel-
       ligence-experts-salaries.html

54.   The Race For AI: Google, Baidu, Intel, Apple In A Rush To Grab
       Artificial Intelligence Startups. (2017, October 25). *CB Insights.* Re-
       trieved from http://www.cbinsights.com/research/top-acquirers-
       ai-startups-ma-timeline/

55. Tilley, A. (2017, April 24). The Great AI Recruitment War: Amazon Is On Top, And Apple Is Almost Nowhere To Be Seen. *Forbes*. Retrieved from http://www.forbes.com/sites/aarontilley/2017/04/18/the-great-ai-recruitment-war-amazon-is-on-top-and-apple-is-almost-nowhere-to-be-seen/

56. Zhou, A. (2017, November 21). Key Qualities To Look For In AI And Machine Learning Experts. *Forbes*. Retrieved from https://www.forbes.com/sites/adelynzhou/2017/11/21/key-qualities-to-look-for-in-ai-and-machine-learning-experts/#2b0d76b565e8

57. Interview with Abhi Jha, Director of Advanced Analytics at McKesson. Interview conducted by Mariya Yao on September 28, 2017.

58. Jia, M. (2017, November 01). Enterprise AI Companies | Business Intelligence Solutions. *TopBots*. Retrieved from http://www.topbots.com/essential-landscape-overview-enterprise-artificial-intelligence/

59. Press, G. (2016, May 01). Data Scientists Spend Most of Their Time Cleaning Data. Retrieved from: http://whatsthebigdata.com/2016/05/01/data-scientists-spend-most-of-their-time-cleaning-data/

60. Baran, B., Di, W., Li, M., & Yuan, C.-Y. (2018, March 6). Big data analytics and machine learning techniques to drive and grow business. Symposium conducted at the Strata Data Conference, San Jose.

61. Andreessen, M. (2011, August 20). Why Software Is Eating the World [Editorial]. *Wall Street Journal*. Retrieved from https://www.wsj.com/articles/SB10001424053111903480904576512250915629460

62. Gold, R., & Chaudhuri, S. (2017, September 28). 'Amazon Effect' Leads Investors to Sour on Global Retail. *Wall Street Journal*. Retrieved from http://www.wsj.com/articles/amazon-effect-leads-investors-to-sour-on-retail-1506591003

63. Perez, S. (2016, November 3). Amazon's private label brands are taking over market share. *Tech Crunch*. Retrieved from http://techcrunch.com/2016/11/03/amazons-private-label-brands-are-killing-it-says-new-report/

64. Herrman, J. (2016, April 17). Media Websites Battle Faltering Ad Revenue and Traffic. *The New York Times*. Retrieved from http://www.nytimes.com/2016/04/18/business/media-websites-battle-falteringad-revenue-and-traffic.html

65. Ibid.

66. Target to Build and Manage New Target.com Platform [Press Release]. (2009, August 7). *Business Wire*. Retrieved from http://www.businesswire.com/news/home/20090807005049/en

67. Hiner, J. (2010, May 11). IT's new holy grail: Break out of the 70% maintenance loop. Retrieved from: http://www.techrepublic.com/blog/tech-sanity-check/its-new-holy-grail-break-out-of-the-70-maintenance-loop/

68. Metz, C. (2017, October 17). Artificial Intelligence Is Setting Up the Internet for a Huge Clash With Europe. *Wired*. Retrieved from http://www.wired.com/2016/07/artificial-intelligence-setting-internet-huge-clash-europe/

69. Metz, C. (2017, October 17). Artificial Intelligence Is Setting Up the Internet for a Huge Clash With Europe. *Wired*. Retrieved from http://www.wired.com/2016/07/artificial-intelligence-setting-internet-huge-clash-europe/

70. Jain, A. (2016, June 29). How Netflix Saves $1 Billion A Year Using AI. Value Walk. Retrieved from http://www.valuewalk.com/2016/06/netflix-how-saves-1-billion-year-ai/

71. Peloton Boosts its Service with 25% SelfService Resolution. (2017, September). *Solvvy*. Retrieved from http://solvvy.com/wp-content/uploads/2017/09/peleton-case-study.pdf

72.   Power, B. (2017, May 30). How Harley-Davidson Used Artificial Intelligence to Increase New York Sales Leads by 2,930%. *Harvard Business Review.* Retrieved from http://hbr.org/2017/05/how-harley-davidson-used-predictive-analytics-to-increase-new-york-sales-leads-by-2930

73.   Interview with Craig Muraskin, Managing Director of Innovation at Deloitte, and Rajeev Ronanki, Principal of Life Sciences and Healthcare at Deloitte. Conducted by Adelyn Zhou on September 20, 2017.

74.   Interview with Jonathan Crane, Chief Commercial Officer at IP-Soft. Conducted by Adelyn Zhou on April 20, 2017.

75.   Interview with Craig Muraskin, Deloitte Managing Director at U.S. *Innovation Group Deloitte.* Conducted by Adelyn Zhou on September 20 2017.

76.   Laskowski, N. (2017, June 15). Measuring ROI for AI investments? Put on your venture capitalist hat. Tech Target. Retrieved from http://searchcio.techtarget.com/news/450420866/Measuring-ROI-for-AI-investments-Put-on-your-venture-capitalist-hat

77.   [Gagan Biyani]. (2013, January 09). Chamath Palihapitiya - how we put Facebook on the path to 1 billion users [Video file]. Retrieved from https://www.youtube.com/watch?v=raIUQP71SBU

78.   From 0 to $1B - Slack's Founder Shares Their Epic Launch Strategy. (n.d.) *First Round Review.* Retrieved from http://firstround.com/review/From-0-to-1B-Slacks-Founder-Shares-Their-Epic-Launch-Strategy/

79.   Fiscal year. (n.d.). In *Wikipedia.* Retrieved November 16, 2017, from http://en.*wikipedia*.org/wiki/Fiscal_year

80.   Koehrsen, W. (2018, March 03). Beyond Accuracy: Precision and Recall. Toward Data Science. Retrieved at https://towardsdatascience.com/beyond-accuracy-precision-and-recall-3da06bea9f6c

81.   Johnson, L. (2017, May 18). Saatchi LA Trained IBM Watson to Write Thousands of Ads for Toyota. *Ad Week*. Retrieved from http://www.adweek.com/digital/saatchi-la-trained-ibm-watson-to-write-thousands-of-ads-for-toyota/

82.   Interview with Anand Rao, Innovation Lead for US Analytics at PwC. Conducted by Adelyn Zhou in 2017.

83.   Sculley, D., Holt, G., Golovin, D., Davydov, E., Phillips, T., Ebner, D., ...Dennison, D. (2015). Hidden Technical Debt in Machine Learning Systems. In C. Cortes, D. D. Lee, M. Sugiyama, and R. Garnett (Eds.), Proceedings of the 28th International Conference on Neural Information Processing Systems - Volume 2. MIT Press, Cambridge, MA, USA, 2503-2511

84.   Sculley, D., Holt, G., Golovin, D., Davydov, E., Phillips, T., Ebner, D., ...Young, M. (2014). Machine Learning: The High Interest Credit Card of Technical Debt. Presented at SE4ML: Software Engineering for Machine Learning (NIPS 2014 Workshop), Montréal, Canada, December 8-13. Retrieved from http://research.google.com/pubs/pub43146.html

85.   Sculley, D., Holt, G., Golovin, D., Davydov, E., Phillips, T., Ebner, D., ...Dennison, D. (2015). *Hidden Technical Debt in Machine Learning Systems*. In C. Cortes, D. D. Lee, M. Sugiyama, and R. Garnett (Eds.), Proceedings of the 28th International Conference on Neural Information Processing Systems - Volume 2. MIT Press, Cambridge, MA, USA, 2503-2511. Retrieved from http://papers.nips.cc/paper/5656-hidden-technical-debt-in-machine-learning-systems.pdf

86.   Kirk, M. (2017, June 8). What is machine learning debt? *O'Reilly*. Retrieved from http://www.oreilly.com/ideas/what-is-machine-learning-debt

87.   Tepper, F. (2016, July 18). Uber has completed 2 billion rides. *Tech Crunch*. Retrieved from http://techcrunch.com/2016/07/18/uber-has-completed-2-billion-rides/

88. Herrman, J. & Del Balso, M. (2017, October 16). Meet Michelangelo: Uber's Machine Learning Platform. Retrieved from http://eng. uber.com/michelangelo/

89. Dunn, J. (2016, May 6). Introducing FBLearner Flow: Facebook's AI backbone. Retrieved from http://code.facebook.com/posts/1072626246134461/introducing-fblearner-flow-facebook-s-ai-backbone/

90. Legal Executive Institute. (2016, January 11). The Size of the US Legal Market: Shrinking Piece of a Bigger Pie — an LEI Graphic. Thompson Reuters. Retrieved from http://www.legalexecutiveinstitute.com/the-size-of-the-us-legal-market-shrinking-piece-of-a-bigger-pie-an-lei-graphic/

91. Gartner. (n.d.). Advance Your Contract Management Process. Retrieved from https://www.cebglobal.com/compliance-legal/smb-legal/contract-management-midsized.html

92. Marciano, J. (2017, June 10). Automating the Law: A Landscape of Legal AI Solutions. *TopBots*. Retrieved from https://www.topbots.com/automating-the-law-a-landscape-of-legal-a-i-solutions/

93. Ambrogi, R. (2017, January 17). ROSS AI Plus Wexis Outperforms Either Westlaw or LexisNexis Alone, Study Finds [blog post]. Law Sites. Retrieved from https://www.lawsitesblog.com/2017/01/ross-artificial-intelligence-outperforms-westlaw-lexisnexis-study-finds.html

94. Sorenson, C. (2017, January 16). Big Law Is Having Its Uber Moment. *MacLean's*. Retrieved from http://www.macleans.ca/economy/business/big-law-is-having-its-uber-moment/

95. Marciano, J. (2017, June 10). Automating the Law: A Landscape of Legal AI Solutions. *TopBots*. Retrieved from https://www.topbots.com/automating-the-law-a-landscape-of-legal-a-i-solutions/

96. Warden, P. (2017, November 13). Deep Learning Is Eating Software [blog post]. Retrieved from https://petewarden.com/2017/11/13/deep-learning-is-eating-software/

97.   Karpathy, A. (2017, November 11). Software 2.0. *Medium*. Retrieved from https://medium.com/@karpathy/software-2-0-a64152b37c35

98.   Lo Giudice, D., Mines, C., LeClair, A., Curran, R., & Homan, A. (2016, October 13). How AI Will Change Software Development and Applications. *Forrester.* Retrieved from https://reprints.forrester.com/#/assets/2/108/'RES121339'/reports

99.   Captain, S. (2017, July 06). West Elm's New AI Tool Scans Pinterest to Recommend Furnishings. *Fast Company*. Retrieved from https://www.fastcompany.com/40437412/west-elms-new-ai-tool-scans-pinterest-to-recommend-furnishings

100.   Cotrupe, J. (2016, April 22). Conversational A.I.: It's A Bot Time for a New Conversation on Customer Engagement (Report # D564-00-EA. Frost & Sullivan. 2016. Retrieved from https://goo.gl/dKvxus.

101.   Salesforce Research. (2017, January 05). Second Annual State of Service: Insights and trends from over 2,600 global service trailblazers. Retrieved from https://a.sfdcstatic.com/content/dam/www/ocms-backup/assets/pdf/misc/state-of-service-e-book-2017.pdf

102.   Witcher, B., Wigder, Z. D., Leggett, K., & Katz, R. (2014, October 29). Good Alone, Better Together: Integrating Chat And Virtual Agents. Forrester. https://www.forrester.com/report/Good+Alone+Better+Together+Integrating+Chat+And+Virtual+Agents/-/E-RES119022

103.   Lee, K.-F. (2018, February 21). Tech companies should stop pretending AI won't destroy jobs. *MIT Technology Review*. Retrieved from https://www.technologyreview.com/s/610298/tech-companies-should-stop-pretending-ai-wont-destroy-jobs/

104.   Executive Office of the President. (2016, December). Artificial Intelligence, Automation, and the Economy. Retrieved from https://www.whitehouse.gov/sites/whitehouse.gov/files/images/EMBARGOED%20AI%20Economy%20Report.pdf

105. Executive Office of the President. (2016, December). Artificial Intelligence, Automation, and the Economy. Retrieved from https://www.whitehouse.gov/sites/whitehouse.gov/files/images/EMBARGOED%20AI%20Economy%20Report.pdf

106. Shook, E., & Knickrehm, M. (2018). Reworking the Revolution. Accenture Strategy. Retrieved from https://www.accenture.com/us-en/company-reworking-the-revolution-future-workforce

107. Interview with Paul Daugherty, CTIO at Accenture. Conducted by Mariya Yao on March 22, 2018.

108. Interview with Paul Daugherty, CTIO at Accenture. Conducted by Mariya Yao on March 22, 2018.

109. Yao, M. (2018, April 05). Responsible AI: Should Smart Machines Be Intrinsically Pro Human? *TopBots*. Retrieved from https://www.topbots.com/responsible-ai-paul-daugherty-james-wilson-accenture-interview/

110. Knowledge@Wharton & Mphasis. (2018, March 01). The Future of Jobs in the World of AI and Robotics. *Knowledge@Wharton*. Retrieved from http://knowledge.wharton.upenn.edu/article/future-jobs-world-ai-robotics/

111. Automation and anxiety. (2016, June 25). *The Economist*. Retrieved from https://www.economist.com/news/special-report/21700758-will-smarter-machines-cause-mass-unemployment-automation-and-anxiety

112. AI Will Put 10 Million Jobs at High Risk—More Than Were Eliminated by the Great Recession. (2017, October 06). *CBInsights*. Retrieved from https://www.cbinsights.com/research/jobs-automation-artificial-intelligence-risk/

ACKNOWLEDGEMENTS

We are grateful to all our friends and supporters who have been with us throughout the journey.

To our book team. Our amazing editor Natalia Zhang and team members Julia Bobak, Joseph Mapue, Kristine Kho and Quinn Bass. To those who offered book publishing experience and advice, Heather LeFevre, Marquina Iliev-Piselli and Larry Robertson.

To Rachel Thomas and Jeremy Howard for their incredible work as teachers of AI and their commitment to diversity and inclusion in the field.

To our fearless friends who poured over manuscripts, made invaluable introductions, opened their homes, and were all around cheerleaders for us: Li Jiang, Carlos Bohorquez, Prasanna Gautam, Łukasz Dziekan, Rosen Kalev, Jonathan Wolter, Tina Tang, Anna Ying, Tiffany Kosolcharoen, Ruth Wang, Raviraj Jain, Jack Chua, Jennifer Q. Chen, Lisa Shalett, and Kapil Chhibber.

To our industry partners with whom we are applying

AI to businesses, one company at a time: Rachel Weiss, Samantha Bort, Rachael Johnson, Jake Annear, Stephen Strauss, Denise Cautela, Sanja Partalo, Jessie Womble, Mahesh Ram, Neil Carty, Sandy Carter, Cindy Stevens, Waikit Lau, Arthur Chan, Ben Parr, Steven Kuyan, Alec Lazarescu, Kathryn Hume, Jeff Pulver, Josh Sutton, Karl Bunch, Anand Rao, and Nigel Duffy.

To friends who gave us moral support from picking the best cover designs and to iterating on various book titles: Harry Li, Anastasia Cifuentes, Greg Schwartz, Chloë Bregman, Laura Mignott, Steve Marks, Ian Thiel, Arlene Kim, Sabina Ahuja, Alan Huang, Molly Zee, Eddie Vaca, Edlyn Yuen, Boaz Omanuti, Stefan Krawczyk, Grace Ng, John Forrester, Lian Huang. Jamie Khor, Dennis Yang. Kai-Ting Neo., Maxim Kesin, Jennifer Q. Chen. Lusi Fang Chien, Alan Chiu, Alexei Andreev, Samuel Nesbitt, Sebastien J Park, Kamilah Taylor, Frank Denbow, Li Yin, Jessica Lam, Yang Hong, Andrew Garvin, Danidu Wijekoon, Malcolm Ong, Julia Lil Jennifer Ditthardt, Dhiren Patel, Matt Lock, Michelle Domanico. Anthony Umina Full, Lucy Zang, Joel Burke, William Truong, Huy Nguyen, Joshua Browder, Bradford Toney, Steven Garcia, Emily Hu, Mike K Tung, Lucy Yu, Balu Chandrasekaran, Sam Wen, Jeff Chang, Zack Chang, Dennis Liu, Tyler He, Ren Wang, Emily Wang, Jared Golden, Stephanie Lai, Victor Vazquez, Nirav H. Shah, Erik Madsen, Amanda Upton, Haibo Lu. Polly Israni, Florence Evina-Ze, Nika Shum, Fang

Yuan, Amy Wu, Jeremy Greenberg, Natalie Lin, Ella Grekov, Matthew Wipperman, Jeremy Schreiber, David L Ross, Irene So, Prasanna Gautam, Yuanjian Carla Li, Rose Yan, Diana Wu, Shirley Liu, Carine Carmy, Reva Minkoff Lyttle, Kejia Zhu, Jordan Lee, Shutong Zhang, Olga Yermolenko, Ohnmar Khin, Vicki Mach Nguyen, Jenn Halweil, Zhenya Mirkin, Wendi Zhang, Josh Zheng, Deema Tamimi, Daniyal Hussain, Julie Yen, Monica Heidelberg, Javier Aguera, Erin Elizabeth Finnegan, Ian Chan, Gary Sharma, Nikolay Valtchanov, Pedro Silva, Frank Lee, Luke Liu, Adam Altman, Andy Manoske, Raymond Palmer.

And above all, thank you to our families and partners who support us and inspire us to dream big. Thank you mom, dad, brothers, and Gabriel, Jin, and Steve. We couldn't have done it without you.

AUTHOR AND EDITOR BIOGRAPHIES

Mariya Yao

Mariya is the Chief Technology and Product Officer at Metamaven, a company that builds machine learning solutions to drive business growth. As an AI designer, Mariya helps executives gain mastery over technical concepts and effectively leverage machine intelligence to transform businesses and society. She's also passionate about promoting diversity and inclusion in STEM education and careers. Mariya speaks internationally at conferences like CES and SxSW, writes for Forbes about the interplay of human and machine intelligence, and is Editor-In-Chief of TOPBOTS, the largest publication and community for enterprise AI professionals.

Through her companies Metamaven and TOPBOTS, Mariya partners with leading global companies such as Google, Baidu, IBM Watson, L'Oreal, PayPal, and LinkedIn to drive strategy, implementation, education, and organizational design for enterprise AI. Prior to Metamaven, she was Founder & Creative Director at

Xanadu, a design and innovation firm building emerging technologies in mobile and IoT for global corporations. She studied Computer Science and Mathematics at Duke University.

Adelyn Zhou

Adelyn is recognized as a leader in marketing and artificial intelligence (AI) by publications including Forbes, Entrepreneur, Inc., Wired, and IBM Watson. She has led growth efforts at Amazon (Quidsi), Eventbrite, TOPBOTS, and Nextdoor. She is a marketing advisor to SignalFire's portfolio of companies and a mentor to startups incubated at NYU Tandon Future Labs and IBM's AI XPRIZE. She is an internationally acclaimed speaker at conferences such as SXSW, CES, Inbound, MarTech, DLD, and more. Adelyn graduated from Harvard College and received her MBA from Harvard Business School.

Marlene Jia

Marlene is the CEO of Metamaven and works with global customers such as L'Oreal, WPP, and PayPal on their enterprise automation initiatives. Her expertise in enterprise software and best practices helps corporations successfully evaluate, develop, and integrate emerging technologies. Prior to Metamaven, she built go-to-market sales teams at high-growth companies Wizeline and Ustream (acq. by IBM) and was COO of Xanadu, a leading strategy and design firm in emerging technology. She's recognized by INC and Entrepreneur as a top keynote speaker and AI expert. Marlene studied economics at Northwestern University, where she started her first multi-million dollar company. She's been a serial entrepreneur ever since.

Natalia Zhang

As an editor and translator, Natalia is dedicated to facilitating communication between audiences with diverse expertise, interests, and backgrounds. Other books that she has edited include *The Political Battle of Sexes* by Leslie Caughell (Rowman & Littlefield, 2016) and *Acting Chinese: An Intermediate-Advanced Course in Chinese Behavioral Culture* by Carolyn Kun-Shan Lee et al. (Taylor & Francis Group, scheduled for publication summer 2019). As a political scientist publishing under her legal name, Wenshuo Zhang, her research investigates how political attitudes and behaviors may change based on whether people used a native language versus a second language to interact with each other. Her most recent project utilizes natural language processing to analyze newspaper data for tone of coverage. Natalia received her PhD from the University of Illinois at Urbana-Champaign and both her MA in East Asian Studies and her BA in Computer Science from Duke University.

70121676R00135

Made in the USA
Columbia, SC
19 August 2019